Going Deeper
in the
Fruit of the Spirit:

Going Deeper
in the
Fruit of the Spirit:

Cultivating Godly Character

Douglas L. Mead, MSSW

XULON PRESS

Xulon Press
2301 Lucien Way #415
Maitland, FL 32751
407. 339. 4217
www.xulonpress.com

Paperback ISBN-13: 978-1-66285-558-0
Ebook ISBN-13: 978-1-66285-559-7

Praise For
Going Deeper in the Fruit of the Spirit: Cultivating Godly Character

"This book is incredibly organized and very easy to follow along. Readers will have no questions regarding what the author shares with them, but they will be intrigued and most likely ask themselves questions on how to better themselves as followers of God. I like how the author focuses on nine godly qualities (love, joy, peace, patience, kindness, goodness, faithfulness, gentleness, and self-control) and really expands upon each one. These qualities are truly the essence of God. It is very refreshing to read how encouraging the author is to his readers. Mr. Mead's no-nonsense and truthful statements challenge the reader's mind and stimulate the soul to ultimately be the fruit God so longs for His children to be."

—Manuscript Review Editor
Xulon Press

"I enjoyed reading this book and thinking about each quality in the list of the Fruit of the Spirit in Galatians 5:22–23 and how I can improve in experiencing them in my life and relationships. This book is sure to encourage everyone to think more deeply about how we understand this passage of Scripture. It is an appeal to consider how the Holy Spirit works in our lives and how we can partner with Him to deepen the genuine experience of having these godly qualities manifested in our Christian walk."

—Jack Conlin, CPA, CGMA
Retired, Director of Corporate Finance,
The Salvation Army Southern Territory

"My friend, Doug Mead, in his latest book, *Going Deeper in the Fruit of the Spirit*, serves as a tour guide who allows us to see inside his own journey to become a fruitful Christian. He takes us by the hand and shows us the open doors he finds most profitable. His words will have strong appeal to people who are logical thinkers and who want to analyze what it means to have the fruits of the Spirit.

"Doug takes us on a thorough journey into the doctrinal issues about whether the fruits of the Spirit are only the work of God or whether it involves some human effort. Doug sides with the second group. In this doctrinal study, he champions personal responsibility, free will, and our partnership with God, putting 'each of us behind the steering wheel of our own lives.'

"On the journey, Doug exposes us to a host of biblical passages and leads us carefully through a deep discussion of all nine fruits of the Spirit, including a fascinating discussion of the difference between joy and happiness. He does not move too fast or lose us in the thickets of theology but offers clear guidance on what the Bible tells us. Those who allow Doug to lead them will find themselves more fully engaged with these 'nine character traits,' better known as the fruits of the Spirit."

—Harold Shank, PhD
Friend and Admirer of Doug Mead
Preached the gospel for over fifty years
Served as President of Ohio Valley University
University Professor and Prolific Author
Recent Book: *Listen and Make Room–Joining God in Welcoming Children*

Previous Book by Douglas L. Mead, MSSW

Going Deeper with God

Addressing Challenging Issues in Our Relationship with God

This book is based on the premise that having a proper and strong relationship with God should be our highest priority. This book is about strengthening faith and helping people come to terms with confusing and controversial topics influencing our understanding of our relationship with God. All of this is not easy to figure out. Some of the obstacles come from the influence of misguided doctrines of some churches and Christian movements. There is a fair amount of discrepancy between what many Christians want from God versus what God actually does. And so, this book is a way to dig deeper in exploring many issues surrounding the nature of the kind of relationship we can have with God.

There are nineteen chapters in this 278-page book focusing on a wide variety of topics. The book includes information on compelling reasons to believe in God and how to enter into a relationship with God. It identifies how this relationship is different than any other relationship we have. It addresses the nature of the intimate relationship we can have with God. It addresses the ramifications of what it means to be created in God's image. It explains the partnership relationship God wants to have and the wonderful ways God can be pleased with us. The book challenges the notion of whether God wants to control all that happens and explores the meaning of the sovereignty of God. It examines the concept of the free will of mankind and the nature of our relationship with the Holy Spirit. It explores the notion of how God speaks to us today. It concludes with chapters on the idea of whether God has a specific plan for our lives and how we can maintain our faith in the midst of suffering.

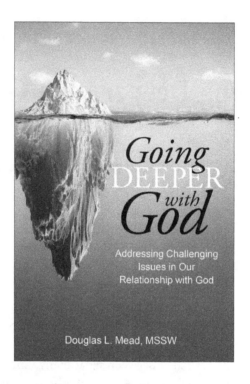

We are confident you will find this book well worth reading. The feedback we are receiving from those who have read it has been very positive. They mention it is easy to read as well as being very thought-provoking. One scholarly minister and motivational speaker called it "brilliant!" One seasoned Christian, Sally Shank, who reviewed the book wrote, "We live in a world of confusing messages. Doug has spent time researching and studying many issues that will help us in our spiritual journey and relationship with God. This is not a book just to be read; this is a book to be studied." Another longtime elder in the church mentioned how he agreed with everything in the book and said everyone should read it.

Dedication

To my loving wife, Nancy,
who served as my sounding
board and encouraged me
all along in the process
of writing this book. In
addition, she also invested
many hours in proof
reading and offered many
great suggestions.

Also, we both would
like to acknowledge our
grandchildren who bring us
much joy and inspiration:

Isaac, Lizzie, Daniel, and
Kaylee.

Contents

INTRODUCTION

Taking a Different Approach

Clues for Understanding This Book

I chose to write on the topic of the "fruit of the Spirit" because of how incredibly important these character traits are for Christians. The challenge for each of us to become more like God in our attitudes, behavior, and character is something we all must earnestly pursue. The nine qualities the apostle Paul identifies as fruit of the Spirit in Galatians 5:22–23 reflect aspects of the nature of God. These are neatly packaged in this passage to inspire us to incorporate these qualities into our lives. In fact, the Scriptures repeatedly mention the need for us to clothe ourselves with these traits. This alone should clue us in on how important they are.

In my research, I have found there are different ways to approach a meaningful discussion on these nine qualities (the fruit) and how we produce them in our lives. There is tremendous diversity of thought when it comes to the topic of how the Holy Spirit works in our lives today. After reading many books and listening to many sermons on YouTube about the "Fruit of the Spirit," I have discovered that many preachers and scholarly people make declarations about the role of the Holy Spirit which can't be supported by Scripture. They give their opinions as if there is no doubt they could be wrong. These kinds of opinions are rarely explained as to what they mean. We'll explore some of this.

What often frustrates me as I listen to sermons and read Christian books is how presenters and writers often do not take the time to explain the phrases and key words they use, such as, "God is in control," "God will provide," "Just give it to God," and "God has a plan for me." They often just say the word or phrase and leave it there. Whether or not they are, these phrases can sound like profound spiritual insights. However, if they are not explained, no one can ultimately know what the person means when they are mentioned. This is largely because many phrases have multiple meanings. I have identified several examples of this in this book. One of my intentions is to communicate by explaining the meaning of the key words, phrases, and terms I am using. I hope I do this well! I wish others would do the same.

Having the notion of "going deeper" into the topics of my books does not mean they are complicated to read. On the contrary, my books are easy reading. This is one of the frequent comments I am receiving about them. I take challenging topics and discuss them in common sense language, not the kind of complicated and technical language some biblical scholars and college professors use. I present information based upon practical views of the subject matter. One should have no trouble understanding the issues I address. Even so, the books are sure to cause everyone to think deeper about the topics addressed.

Providing Something Different, New and More

When deciding to write this book on the topic of the fruit of the Spirit, I began first by asking, "Do I have something different, new, or more to add to the roster of current books and articles available on this topic?" I discovered I have much to add by offering this book.

One issue I found is that most of the books and articles, which are easy to find, seem to be written by authors who overstate the role of the Holy Spirit in our lives. These books and articles misconstrue the extent of our involvement versus the Holy Spirit's in the development of the fruit. They assert the Holy Spirit has a sole, controlling, and overriding role in the development of the fruit in our lives. This comes from the belief many have that "God takes control of everything," which comes from their particular understanding of the sovereignty of God.

In contrast to this, there are other widespread views, similar to mine, which understand and affirm the value of independent free will and how to balance this with the role of the Holy Spirit. This is opposed to the viewpoint which forwards the idea that God is in control of everything. Free will encompasses the notion that God delegates power to human beings to use their abilities to impact the outcomes of their efforts. We have independent or libertarian free will, which means our will is self-determined. We have the ability to choose otherwise than what God or how anyone else might want us to choose. Free will embraces the notion that we are to do our best to follow the Scriptures with the help of the Holy Spirit. Unfortunately, books and articles written from this perspective on the topic of the fruit of the Spirit are difficult to find.

Another issue I found is regarding how each of the fruit is often discussed in books and articles. This book will go into greater detail in understanding the nature of each of the fruit mentioned in Galatians 5:22–23. It will provide a practical view of how we generate the godly attributes the fruit represent and how we apply them to our lives. It will highlight the responsibility we have for our thoughts, actions, decisions, and the values we hold dear. It will offer suggestions on how to overcome obstacles we face as we seek to grow in the maturing of the fruit.

Another area of difference is the notion I forward in this book regarding the partnership relationship we have with God. This is largely overlooked or downplayed in the other books and articles on this topic. This may be somewhat controversial to some, but I believe this is a very important concept to understand and celebrate in the relationship we have with our Creator.

During the time of COVID restrictions on in-person church attendance, I turned to the internet to listen to various sermons in addition to the ones from my church. I came across a pastor who did an outstanding job preaching on the topic of our partnership relationship with God. It was very refreshing. I called him up, introduced myself, and we spoke for more than an hour discussing the merits of this biblical concept. I told him I wondered why we didn't hear more sermons and teachings on this topic. He agreed we should be hearing more teaching on this topic.

Another area of difference with other books and articles is the distinctive perspective and background from which I approach this topic. As my training and professional career is in the social service field, I bring a broader outlook and more practical perspective to the discussion of how we understand and apply the fruit mentioned in Galatians 5:22–23. I will provide many interesting insights to topics based upon my professional counseling background and experiences.

Critical Thinking and Dealing with Disagreements

Have you ever met anyone who thinks exactly as you do? Do you have a friend who has all the same views and opinions, including understanding the Scriptures exactly as you do? How about what we know about biblical scholars? Do they all understand and interpret the Scriptures the same way? Obviously, the answer to all these questions is no! We must understand that this is the reality in which we do Bible studies.

It is good to get a variety of perspectives on topics and respectfully address the disagreements we have with others, including the reasons why. I believe this is something to embrace and not shy away from, generally speaking. Writing on Christian topics can be very challenging because there are so many differing beliefs, doctrines, and denominational biases which come to bear on many topics. Much of this comes from the way people interpret Scriptures differently. It's hard to avoid having disagreements on many biblical topics. On the positive side, these discussions will only help us think more deeply about issues and cause us to want to study further to confirm or clarify our own understanding.

It is good for Christians to consider many sides of an issue, especially when they represent important information to know. Again, we should not shy away from reading material just because we may not agree on some issues. These will actually help us clarify our own viewpoints. I often intentionally read books when I expect to disagree with the authors in order to better understand their viewpoints and clarify and reaffirm mine. This is a healthy exercise.

Some areas we may disagree on with other Christian believers could relate to aspects of an issue we have not fully explored. Sometimes we have blind spots and don't even know what we don't know. Again, we have much to gain by considering other points of view, even if we aren't sure we agree.

Being able to deal with alternative viewpoints is one of the most important elements of critical thinking. Weighing the arguments on different sides of an issue and coming to a conclusion regarding one's own viewpoint is the essence of critical thought. Thinking deeper is, in part, accomplished by asking probing questions and doing research in the quest to attain clearer understanding.

For those who would disagree with my perspective on how we develop the godly traits in Galatians 5, there is still much in this book that will be very helpful. So, don't let any disagreement discourage you from reading this book, especially the chapters on each of the nine qualities or character traits the fruit represent.

Finding Common Ground

All Christians should acknowledge the authority of the Scriptures when it comes to dealing with spiritual issues. As many say, show me the book, chapter, and verse for the point you are making so we can see how closely it correlates to the Scriptures. Most of us can also appreciate that understanding Scripture can be a challenging task at times. There are many reasons why this is so. One is simply that some Scriptures are just hard to understand. How many times do we say, "Okay, that sounds great, but what does it mean?"

There are other paraphrased and easy English versions of the Bible that try to make the text less complicated to understand. These can be helpful, but we must realize the limitations of these versions as they often vary from the exact meaning of the original language, that is, Hebrew or Greek. Some of these versions include: The Message (MSG), The Living Bible, New Living Translation (NLT), The Amplified Bible, and The Phillips Translation. Even though each of the paraphrased and amplified versions of the Scriptures may have the word "Bible" in their book title, this does not give their words the authority of Scripture.

Unfortunately, there are many preachers who employ these paraphrased versions in their sermons to manipulate the meaning of Scripture so it can be used to convey what they want it to say. They do this by finding Scriptures in these versions that use specific words they are looking for but which are not in the original language. So instead, they use the paraphrased versions to get around that obstacle. When understanding the Bible, words matter a lot. Thankfully, the internet provides ways to look up the Greek and Hebrew words used in the Bible so we can check on the accuracy of what the original biblical writers were intending to express.

You will notice I define several Greek words used in the Scriptures in this book. That's because accurately understanding what a key word means is very important. I use the Interlinear Bible at the "Biblehub.com/interlinear/" website for this information.

Another guideline we should acknowledge and agree on is the use of godly logic. Norman Geisler and Ronald Brooks, in their book, *Come Let us Reason: An Introduction to Logical Thinking*, make the case for how important logic is to our lives and in how we can use logic to help us understand the intent of Scripture. [1] These efforts are sometimes undervalued. Being logical is one of the primary attributes of God. God is a rational being, and all the principles of good reason flow from His very nature. We must seek to honestly and humbly pursue truth. False or misleading understandings can have serious consequences. Logic provides a filter to use in understanding the veracity of concepts and doctrines. If something does not meet the test of godly logic, it should be questioned carefully for being accurate.

Logic gives us rules (laws) on how we process and express information and how to make good decisions. It draws us like a magnet to make right conclusions. Living logically is the only way to live life most effectively. Without logic being applied, there can be no rational discussion of anything. The main point here is that Scripture and Christian doctrine should be logical and rational. This is especially true as it takes into consideration the character of God and how God works in our lives, including how the spirit world influences our lives. It is important to assert that we are referring to godly logic. This takes into consideration God's perspective and what He is trying to teach us.

Uniting with Divinity

The assertion will be made in this book that the nine qualities of the fruit of the Spirit identified in Galatians 5:22–23 are actually attributes of God. They are part of His divine nature. Therefore, we become more like Christ and more like God every day by having these qualities increase and mature in our lives. Becoming more like God is one of the great goals of the Christian life. It is from God's attributes that we can understand our purpose in life. This purpose must align with having an increasing amount of God's qualities present in our lives as we were created to be like God.

We know the passage in Galatians is just one of the places where we find appeals to develop these godly qualities in our lives. There are additional passages found throughout the New Testament that mention the same and similar qualities stated by the same author and others. In fact, there are several additional qualities emphasized in these other passages that deserve our attention as well. This includes 2 Peter 1:3–11, Colossians 3:12–15, Colossians 1:19–20, Ephesians 4:2–3, 2 Peter 3:10–12, Galatians 6:9–10, and Titus 2:11–14. It is interesting to note that in these verses, the phrase "of the Spirit" is not mentioned as it is in Galatians 5:22–23. The question is, "Why not? "This is something worth thinking about." So taken together, including the fruit of the Spirit, these passages mention the following godly qualities: love, joy, peace, patience, kindness, goodness, faithfulness, gentleness, self-control, knowledge, godliness, perseverance, compassion, humility, forgiveness, and thankfulness. However, for the purposes of this book, we will only explore the first nine qualities listed here.

A Word about Character

Followers of Jesus need to be different from those who are non-believers. Character is one of the most important areas in which this difference should be noticeable.

We can choose the kind of character we want to have. That is because a person's character is not a static or unchanging expression of who we are as an individual for all time. The fruit of the Spirit qualities are a prime example of target goals we should strive to achieve in our lives. This relates to how we must spend substantial time and effort to learn and grow in these qualities.

Thankfully, our character is never set in stone. If that were true, there would be no hope for those who want to improve themselves or change the direction of their lives. The character of a person is a snapshot picture in time of who a person is deep down. Character is developed through a lifelong process of learning and personal growth. Character can be influenced negatively or positively by the relationships we have with significant others in our lives. This underscores why it is best for people to surround themselves with other Christians who can be a constructive influence in their lives.

Does the Fruit Refer to One's Character or to One's Attitudes?

This is a good question. After I had finished the manuscript for this book, I found a sermon by John MacArthur on the "Fruit of the Spirit, Part 1," posted on YouTube. He is one of the prominent spiritual leaders in the Calvinist movement today. In his sermon, he was emphatic to label the fruit as "attitudes."[2] This took me aback as I was viewing the fruit as godly character traits. Having given this further thought, I am going to stay with my original view on this. Yes, a point can be made that character and attitudes have similarities. They share some of the same qualities. However, I agree with many others who say that there is a significant difference between them.

Simply stated, attitudes are about an outward focus, whereas character is inward. Attitudes are choices we make toward specific issues. Character relates to our identity and nature. Attitudes are focused on opinions regarding matters that can change in the short term. Character is not about likes and dislikes of a given topic or a situation. It relates to a person's deeper qualities. Attitudes can change easily and quickly. Character does not change in the short term and is about our values and qualities, which run deep. Attitudes are easy to detect, whereas character takes a much longer and deeper analysis. Attitude is about making short-term judgment calls, whereas character is about deeper, enduring, and guiding qualities.

Another important perspective here is how the qualities of the fruit relate to God. I don't believe we would say that these are just the attitudes of God. These are much deeper and relate to the character of God. These come from who God is deep down where we know they are prominent and lasting qualities of God we all can depend on. As part of God's nature, these are permanent qualities of God.

For real and lasting change within a person, we want to deal at the level of one's character. So, that's where we will focus as we cultivate the fruit of the Spirit mentioned in Galatians 5:22–23.

A Word about Godliness

Although the words "godly" and "godliness" appear only twenty-four-times in the New Testament, the case can be made that the entire Bible is a book on godliness. Godliness is about being like God. It's about being like Jesus Christ. It's about what we all should strive to be as Christians. It's the essence of the Christian life.

The Greek word for godliness is **eusebeia** (εὐσέβεια), pronounced yoo-seb'-i-ah, which has the connotation of awe, devotion, and piety (loyalty, dutiful conduct) toward God. Godliness is an inner response to the things of God which shows itself in godly piety. Devotion signifies a life given, or dedicated, to God. [3] Therefore, a godly person is one who has a godly life-style where God is at the center of one's thoughts and actions.

Godliness can be defined as devotion to God which results in a life that is pleasing to God. It is lived out by those who have a pervasive sense of God's presence, a correct concept of God's character, and a constant awareness of our obligations to God. Godliness is also the avoidance of things that we know displease God. These are mentioned in the Scriptures as the "what not to-dos," which often come before the listing of what we should be doing.

Unique Aspects of My Perspective

As I mentioned earlier, a major area in which this book is different than most other books on the topic of the fruit of the Spirit relates to my background from which I approach this topic. I have a unique perspective compared to many other Christian authors. Several years ago I completed a forty-year career in the social service sector. I was a state-licensed clinical social worker and provided professional counseling to those struggling with marital, family, and personal problems from a Christian point of view. In this book, I bring up concepts and processes about personal life issues and interpersonal relationships which others do not as their backgrounds are more limited to religious studies.

One of the reasons I entered the social services profession was because it is based on the positive premise that we can help people change if they so desire. Many are facing difficult challenges and need some help to overcome their issues. My Christian orientation has softened my heart toward those in need and has given me a deeper sense of compassion for all people. It was this passion that motivated my decision to work in the helping profession. My training and experience has taught me much over the years. Insights I've gained from this work have influenced my understanding of the capacity of people to work through their issues and make substantial changes in their lives.

As a result of all of this, I've also come to a deeper appreciation of what it means for mankind to be created in God's own image (Gen. 1: 27). The vast amount of ability God has given to each of us at creation enables us to accomplish a great deal. Human beings are extremely complex. We have the cognitive ability (brain power) to handle tremendous challenges. We learn how to cope with life from our very beginnings (birth) thanks to our parents and involved relatives. As we mature, we learn to accomplish incredible tasks. We have an emotional side to us, which is like a sixth sense. This helps us understand and be more alert and sensitive to differing sides of issues. We can be incredibly creative. We can solve complex issues and learn from our mistakes. We possess a sense of self-love and protection. We are social beings who need to be in relationship with others. We have a spiritual side to our nature, which longs for a meaningful relationship with God and finding purpose in life.

Being created by God in His own image is an amazing concept. Not only did the Genesis passage about mankind's creation call it very good

(Gen. 1:31), but there are many Scriptures adding to the idea of how special mankind is in God's eyes. All of creation shows God's glory (Rom. 1:20). We are fearfully and wonderfully made (Ps. 39:14). We find many passages of Scriptures revealing that God and Jesus take joy in us, such as Zephaniah 3:17, where we are told that God takes great delight in us, and in Hebrews 12:2, where we read "For the joy set before Him, He endured the cross..."

So why do I mention all of this, you ask? Well, it's because it relates to how I address a topic like the fruit of the Spirit in Galatians 5:22–23. This passage is a call to establish and grow nine godly qualities or character traits in our lives. My background informs me that people have inherent abilities which can be employed to learn and apply these traits in their lives. Because of this, even non-believers can learn and apply many of these traits if they so desire. We all know loving, kind, and friendly people can show evidence of these qualities even though they are not followers of Christ. As the apostle Paul has written this passage to believers, this will be the perspective for how I will proceed in this book.

We Develop Skills and Mature by Learning

Based on our God-given nature and abilities, we are designed to accomplish much in life. This comes largely from our cognitive capacities given to us at creation, the power of our minds to learn. Everyone's experience of life involves constant learning. We never stop being learners. There are many ways in which we learn. When we are just starting out in life, it is the role of our parents to teach us what we need to know and how to act. As we mature, we learn from the additional teaching from all kinds of people as well as from our experiences. This highlights the way we develop the qualities of the fruit of the Spirit. It is largely through studying, learning, and growing.

We don't just pray to God and expect the Holy Spirit to instantly give us these qualities in full measure. God does not zap us with these qualities at a given point in time. People don't lay hands on us and we miraculously attain the fullness of these qualities. There is no pill that will produce these qualities. God does not use holy hypnosis in activating these qualities. We are not given these qualities as gifts. There are no shortcuts to the development and ongoing application of these qualities in our lives. It is a process of deliberate effort on our part with the help of the Holy Spirit.

Over time, we mature spiritually as a result of all the accumulative learning we've done. Much of this is a result of how much we have learned from our experiences in life. Some say experience is our greatest teacher.

Now I know some will disagree with these assertions. I will highlight and respond to some of these in chapter two. In addition to what I present there, I'd like to briefly provide a couple of other contrary viewpoints to what I just mentioned above.

John MacArthur acknowledged in his sermon on the "Fruit of the Spirit, Part 1" that we are commanded to have the fruit of Galatians 5:22–23 in our lives. He also said that the fruit are all produced by the Holy Spirit, not us. However, he took this a step further by saying, "We are commanded to do only what the Spirit can do in us."[4] He believes the commands are directed to us, but they are the work and responsibility of the Holy Spirit to fulfill. Now, I know of no Scripture that clearly or even faintly supports this notion. This idea is not mentioned any time a direct command is given in the Scriptures. If this notion were true, it would seem to be an important piece of information to have explicitly mentioned and explained in the Scriptures. This idea just seems to stand in defiance of logic. Unfortunately, John MacArthur does not explain why he said this and what he meant by it. He just declared this to be so.

Now, a major premise of my book will be from a contrary perspective. I believe the appeals and commands of Scripture which are directed to us are our responsibility to fulfill. We will be held accountable for fulfilling these in our lives. As a sampling of this, we are told in Titus 2:12 to live self-controlled, upright, and godly lives. The apostle Paul tells Timothy in 1 Timothy 4:7, "Have nothing to do with godless myths and old wives' tales; rather, train yourself to be godly." We are told in 2 Peter 1:5–6, "For this reason, make every effort to add to your faith goodness, and to goodness, knowledge; and to knowledge, self-control; and to self-control, perseverance; and to perseverance, godliness..." Surely these are also directed to us for us to carry out.

As another doctrinal perspective I find troublesome, Michael Caputo, in his book *The Fruits of the Holy Spirit, Understanding the Transforming Fruits of God's Spirit*, contends that all of the fruit mentioned in Galatians 5:22–23 are miraculously given to believers. He asserts they are all gifts from God and not produced by us. He spends much effort to affirm that all believers should regularly expect miracles.

He states the following in his chapter on faith/faithfulness:

> We must believe, in other words, that we can ask for the laws of nature to be broken on our behalf. We must ask for, and must believe that we can have a job, when there are no jobs. We must believe that it is possible to have healing, when we are beyond repair. We must believe that it is possible for cancer to disappear, when it's already spread all over our body. We must believe that God can heal a sick organ, even when doctors say the organ has almost stopped working. We must believe that God can even provide healing for blind eyes and for a paralyzed body, which is scientifically impossible. [5]

He goes on to say, "To ask for the impossible, and believe that it can be possible, we must first ask for the required faith that only God can provide. When that faith is present, then we have the pre-requisite for receiving the impossible."[6]

He then says, "Therefore, first comes total faith, and that is the proof that the impossible <u>will occur</u>. But it is not the kind of faith we produce through mental gymnastics. It is not <u>our</u> faith. <u>It is a gift from God</u>."[7] (All of the underlines provided here as emphasis are his.)

He then goes on to say: "When *total faith* is present, God has given to us the requirement for the impossible to occur. When total faith is present, the impossible <u>will</u> occur; <u>but it is God's doing from beginning to end</u>. This is the type of trust that produces great miracles."[8]

I don't know of any Scriptures that convey these bold statements. One of my fears for those who agree with this thinking, who expect God to do these things, is that they are being set up for great disappointment and disillusionment. This could end up causing them to question or give up on their faith in God.

As one more example, I found a video on YouTube of Pastor Gregory Dickow entitled "The Truth About the Fruit of the Spirit" which premiered on March 12, 2020. [9] Mr. Dickow has a charismatic background and is affiliated with the Word of Faith movement, something I discuss in my first book. He is founder and pastor of Life Changers International Church, a nondenominational megachurch with over 3,000 members. He also has a syndicated television program which airs around the world.[10]

In his message on YouTube he simply said that we are "to eat of the fruit of the Spirit." He said, "You cannot produce what you don't eat." He asked, "What do we do with fruit?" He responded, "We eat it, we don't produce it."

Even though hearing this, it still is difficult to understand what he means. How do we eat a godly quality? Even in his message he was admitting he was having a hard time explaining this idea.

What I see here is someone who is taking a metaphor and applying it literally. The fruit of the Spirit in Galatians 5:22-23 are not edible substances. They are attributes and qualities we strive to become more like everyday.

Again, these three perspectives from John MacArthur, Michael Caputo and Gregory Dickow are prime examples that reveal how Christian people have differing interpretations of Scripture and stand on conflicting biblical doctrines.

Gifts versus Fruit

The apostle Paul discusses gifts of the Spirit or spiritual gifts in several places. These are mentioned in 1 Corinthians 12:7–11, 1 Corinthians 12:27–31, Ephesians 4:7–13, and Romans 12:3–8. These spiritual gifts refer to supernatural and miraculous manifestations of the Holy Spirit in the lives of specific people to whom God chooses to give these gifts. Not everyone has the same gifts. These are abilities given to people for the common good (1 Cor. 12:7).

The "fruit" of the Spirit are different from "gifts" of the Spirit. The fruit is for everyone and is about developing godly character, not being given specific abilities. The fruit mentioned in Galatians 5:22–23 are not gifts of the Spirit with immediate effect. Gifts are given; fruit is developed. Gifts come fully manifested. The fruit take time to be fully cultivated and matured in the lives of believers. The case will be made in this book that the fruit comes from two life streams, us and God.

Hopeful Impact

It is quite obvious the Scriptures put a significant emphasis on the need for Christians to develop many godly qualities as a part of their efforts to become more like God. These passages seek to get us to progress along a personal change process. We are encouraged throughout Scripture to display Christ-like character. This is a process, and it takes time. Actually, it's a lifetime, ongoing pursuit. For Christians, this deserves our devoted attention and best efforts. That's why all Christians should read a book like this!

I hope you will find this book to be very helpful as you seek to enrich and deepen the godly qualities of love, joy, peace, patience, kindness, goodness, faithfulness, gentleness, and self-control in your lives. I also hope the information in this book will inspire your passion for God and that His likeness in you will be clearly seen by all.

So, are you ready to be challenged to think deeper? God bless you as you begin this journey!

CHAPTER 1

Major Insights for Godly Living

The Incredible Impact of the Fruit

"But the fruit of the Spirit is love, joy, peace, patience,
kindness, goodness, faithfulness, gentleness and
self-control."

—Galatians 5:22–23

ATTENTION! If you have not read the introduction, I strongly encourage
you to do so as it provides a helpful foundation for understanding this book.

I imagine you've chosen this book to read because of your particular
interest in this topic, along with a realization this Scripture holds some very
significant insights for godly living. Good choice! This passage provides
insider information on key issues of how God wants us to live. I concur with
you that exploring a deeper understanding of the "fruit of the Spirit" as the
apostle Paul identifies these in Galatians 5:22–23 is a worthy endeavor.

There are a few passages of Scripture that seem to zone right in on what
elevates their importance above others. These passages grab our attention
and compel us to focus on them. As some examples, consider the following:

- The greatest commandment in the Law is... (Matt. 22:37–40)
- So in everything, do to others... (Matt. 7:12)
- But the greatest of these is... (1Cor. 13:14)

1

- Religion that God our Father accepts as pure and faultless is... (James 1:27)
- The only thing that counts is... (Gal. 5:6)

A compelling case can be made that the passage about the fruit of the Spirit in Galatians 5:22–23 is one of enormous importance also. Out of all the appeals and admonitions in the Scriptures, here the apostle Paul provides a short list of specific character traits for us to develop in our lives. Since this passage is written to believers, this then is to whom this book is addressed.

In Galatians 5:22–23, the apostle Paul uses metaphoric language linking the character traits and godly qualities (fruit) to the Holy Spirit. When something is attached to the Holy Spirit, it is also attached directly to God Himself. This is how the apostle Paul elevates the importance of this passage of Scripture.

These nine words in verses 22–23 describe inner character traits, which should strongly influence, if not transform, our lives. Exhibiting these qualities will reflect the scope of the Christ-like nature and godly character present in each of us. We can know God more deeply and clearly by observing His attributes and applying these to our lives.

These nine character traits, when more fully realized, can have a tremendous impact on the world. Some say there is nothing more important to us and the world than the fruit of the Spirit as we share our Christian witness to others. This is likely very true. These qualities reveal evidence we are authentic Christians. Jesus says in Matthew 7:20: "Thus, by their fruit you will recognize them." Our faith will reveal itself by the fruit it produces.

In one sense, these nine Christian virtues are qualities by which people in the world, both non-believers and believers, will judge us. This is because one of the ways in which we manifest our faith and relationship with God is seen in how we act with godly qualities toward others. This relates to the well-known axiom, "Preach the gospel at all times and, if necessary, use words."[11] The way we manifest these nine qualities is powerful evidence of our faith commitment to God.

We can find a similar concept in what was stated years ago in Stephen R. Covey's book, *The 7 Habits of Highly Successful People: Powerful Lessons in Personal Change.*[12] He stated that his research has identified the following concept as being very important: "What we are communicates far more eloquently than anything we say and do." What we are relates to how we act toward others and live our lives.

One of the lessons I learned when retiring and moving to Southern California relates to how challenging it is to get to be known by others. Hardly anyone in California knew the reputation I established where I used to live. One of the things I do early on when meeting new people is to let them know I am a Christian.

Most of us realize that going public with our faith is a powerful way to draw attention to our Christian witness. This puts us in the spotlight. People will be watching us. I find this gives me an opportunity to let them regularly see what my faith means to me. I am expressing and sharing my faith with them every day through my behavior and attitudes.

However, when I let others know this, it is like I have put a bumper sticker on me that says, "I am a Christian and represent our loving God. Watch me so you can see an example of how a born-again child of God should act." That's a lot of pressure!

I am now playing golf regularly, and this is a challenging context in which to showcase one's joy and patience. Enough said! Actually, I hardly ever let it get me upset. I just understand I'm not that good and shouldn't expect to be mistake-free. I just laugh at a bad shot and move on to the next one. (I do a lot of laughing!) I also marvel at the good ones (joy).

In reality, like it or not, our attitudes and behaviors are very noticeable for others to see, no matter the context. We can't hide. We must try to do our best in each of the circumstances in which we find ourselves, remembering we represent our heavenly Father.

Manifesting the fruit of the Spirit in our lives comes with many advantages. It will tremendously benefit our personal relationships, it will strengthen our relationship with God, and it will enrich our individual lives. Based on this and all of what we've already discussed, I believe every Christian would do well to consider it an urgent and vital need to understand and apply this particular passage of Scripture to our lives.

The Need to Understand Symbolic Language in the Bible

Let's briefly discuss the use of symbolic language in the Scriptures. Again, the passage in Galatians 5:22–23 is based on a metaphor. Understanding this will guide us in how we interpret this passage.

We all know that symbolic language is used regularly, both in spoken and written communication. There can be many reasons for a communicator to use figurative language. One may be for effect, to gain one's attention. Another is to help one understand a concept in a deeper way. Another is to make a literal fact more graphic or visual.

Some of the symbolic language used is the following:

- **Simile**—one thing is likened to another dissimilar thing by the use of "like" or "as"[13]
- **Metaphor**—a comparison made between two or more things using figurative language[14]
- **Parable**—a short story usually of a familiar kind similar to an extended simile that reveals truth that, in many ways, the meaning is concealed[15]
- **Analogy**—similarity in some respects between things otherwise unlike, showing how two things are alike[16]
- **Hyperbole**—exaggeration used for effect and not to be taken literally[17]
- **Personification**—a figure of speech in which a thing, quality, or idea is represented as a person; animation of inanimate things[18]
- **Anthropomorphism**—attributing physical characteristics to God[19]
- **Paradox**—a truth that seems contradictory, unbelievable, or absurd, but that may be true in fact[20]

Interpretation of Symbolic Language

We need to carefully distinguish between literal and figurative language. If you are an FBI agent, you may say you want the facts and just the facts. Sometimes we may wish the Scriptures were more direct and explicit, just telling us straight up what we need to know. However, one thing is clear. There is quite a lot of symbolic language used throughout the Scriptures and in our everyday lives. When figurative language is used, we have to be careful and cautious about how we interpret it.

Much symbolic language makes understanding a concept easier. Sometimes it is more complicated and requires more skill of interpretation to understand what is being said. In researching what differing people say about what a passage with symbolic language means, one may find that they often provide different interpretations of the passage. As a word of caution, when we try to understand passages that rely on figurative language, we would do well to be careful not to take a simple message and try to extract too much symbolism from it. Sometimes people go a little too far with this. Also, sometimes people apply literal meaning to figurative passages when they should not do this.

Fruit of the Spirit—A Metaphor

Here in Galatians 5:22–23, Paul uses the metaphor "fruit of the Spirit," but he only provides a partial explanation of the metaphor by identifying what is meant by the fruit. We often see metaphors in passages dealing with the role of the Holy Spirit. We find this in the use of terms, such as "walking" with the Holy Spirit and being "filled" with the Holy Spirit.

In a metaphor, a word denoting one subject of activity is used in place of another to suggest a likeness between them. Metaphors are intended to turn complicated ideas into more simple concepts. They are also used to infuse written texts with vivid descriptions, which make the texts more vibrant and enjoyable to read. [21]

As a metaphor, the phrase "fruit of the Spirit" is often understood to mean what the Holy Spirit produces in a believer. That is why so many who teach and write on this topic put their emphasis on the Holy Spirit playing a primary (and sole) role in the development of these qualities. Now I can understand why many interpret the passage this way. However, we should pause and look more deeply into the nature of this metaphor and the role of the Holy Spirit in our lives to provide guidance here.

What we see are two variables in this metaphor. They are (1) "the fruit," and (2) "of the Spirit." We can turn to the Greek language to get an idea of what is meant by the word "fruit." I use the interlinear Bible website for getting this information. The word in Greek is **karpós** (καρπός).[22] Three words used to define karpós are "deed," "action," and "result." It appears to be focused on the work and results of the fruit. Many would say it is of the Holy Spirit's work. However, the word karpós also has the following words used in the interlinear Bible website to help define it based on the Scripture of John 15:1–8, where Jesus uses fruit as figurative language in the analogy of "the Vine and the Branches."

> *Fruit;* (figuratively) everything done in *true partnership with Christ*, i. e. a believer (a branch) lives in union with Christ (the Vine). By definition, fruit results from *two* life streams—the Lord and us humans working together to yield what is eternal.

From this notion, we can look at karpós as a result of a true partnership with Christ. Therefore, we can surmise that the fruit results from two life streams: us and the Spirit. However, this is a concept that many seem to downplay, which is why I am spending some time to explain this viewpoint.

In the case of the Galatians 5:22–23 passage, we know exactly what the fruit refers to in this metaphor. Paul explicitly gives us the nine character traits the word "fruit" refers to: love, joy, peace, patience, kindness, goodness, faithfulness, gentleness and self-control. As we examine these words, we see they relate to godly qualities, God's character. These are qualities God wants us to develop and increase in measure so we can be more like Him. These are qualities of God's divine nature and quite different from the sinful nature mentioned earlier in Galatians 5.

What can be true and accurate and what also can be somewhat confusing is how we can substitute words that have the same meaning. Words with the same meaning are interchangeable. So, in the first half of the metaphor, we could replace the word "fruit" (karpós) with "godly qualities" or "godly characteristics" or concepts like this and it would mean the same thing. An equivalent procedure can be done to the last half of the metaphor. I propose that the "of the Spirit" phrase in this metaphor can also relate to "of God" or "of God's nature" or concepts like this as God and the Holy Spirit are one and the same.

If we insert these words into the metaphor, we can then phrase this metaphor in a variety of ways or combinations. This can include the following: (1) "godly qualities of the Holy Spirit," (2) "godly qualities of God," (3) "the fruit of God," (4) "the fruit of God's nature" (5) "godly characteristics of the Holy Spirit," or (6) "godly characteristics of God." (It could also include other combinations.) Looking at it from this perspective allows us to see the "fruit of the Spirit" metaphor in a different light. The point is, this passage is more about the godly qualities we are to have, not how we produce them in our lives. It does not have to refer to the idea that it is the Holy Spirit alone who produces the fruit in us. Its focus could simply relate to the notion that the qualities representing the fruit refer to the characteristics of God we must have in our lives.

Previously in the passage, the apostle Paul talks about the acts of the sinful nature and then introduces the qualities of the godly nature we are to have instead. What the sinful nature desires is not what the divine nature desires. Those who belong to Christ have crucified the sinful nature with its passions and desires (Gal. 5:24). Christians live according to a new set of values, qualities and standards. Our passions should flow from our godly nature.

To keep this discussion simple, let's just continue to use the phrase "fruit of the Spirit" from here on out as we look deeply into its meaning and application.

Motivations of This Passage

This passage is written specifically to Christians. It relates to our faith and encourages us to focus on things of the Spirit versus things of the flesh.

So we can ask, "Why did Paul choose to use a metaphor here?" I believe it was for effect, to focus our attention on the nine qualities as standouts from other appeals in the Scriptures. Connecting God to something does give that something extra importance. Here the apostle Paul emphasizes there is something very special about these nine character traits.

However, we all know that these nine virtues are not the only character traits that are important and worthy of our examination. Paul mentions certain qualities in other passages of Scripture. Those godly qualities are important also. The Holy Spirit is with us to help us with those qualities also, even though they are not labeled as fruit of the Spirit.

A case can be made that Paul did not literally elevate the nine qualities in Galatians 5:22–23 as more important than other passages of Scripture. He did not explicitly, in plain words, say this. We must accept that all Scriptures encouraging us to take on certain qualities are important.

Differing Perspectives to This Topic

The varying perspectives on interpreting this passage come from the differing doctrinal or theological perspectives among church denominations, Christian movements, and Christian groups. There are many groups that believe in the extreme notion of the controlling role of God and the Holy

Spirit. It is important to realize that every book, article, internet blog, and written piece one can find is influenced by the doctrinal bias of the author.

It is my hope this book on the fruit of the Spirit will present fresh ideas, offer many insights, and provide a deep dive into this topic. **The greatest benefit of this book will come as it helps all of us to effectively apply these qualities to our lives.**

So yes, having these nine character traits to the highest level of quality possible is what we should all strive for as we walk with Jesus. Falling short in exhibiting any of these qualities should be considered a personal failure worthy of our attention and remediation. I can only believe God is disappointed with us when we fail to exhibit these qualities in ways that bring glory to His name. "This is to my father's glory, that you bear much fruit, showing yourselves to be my disciples" (John 15:8). If we were to be unloving, unkind, mean, hurtful to others, it would no doubt tarnish how we reflect who God is to the world. I say "we fail" as I don't see how we can blame the Holy Spirit for any of our shortcomings as the Holy Spirit never falls short or makes a mistake. We'll discuss this in more detail in the next chapter.

Pursuing Holiness and Perfection

We know there are Scriptures that tell us to be holy and perfect.

- **Matthew 5:48**—Be perfect, therefore, as your heavenly father is perfect.
- **1 Peter 1:15–16**—But just as he who called you is holy, so be holy in all you do; for it is written: "Be holy, because I am holy."
- **Hebrews 12:14**—Make every effort to live in peace with all men and to be holy; without holiness no one will see the Lord.
- **1 Thessalonians 4:7**—For God did not call us to be impure, but to live a holy life.

So, what are we to think about these passages? We can understand that holiness and perfection are nothing less than conformity to the character of God. However, we also understand that we are not God. And so we ask, are we really required to be perfect and holy like God and nothing less? Is that even possible?

When we think about it, we can understand why holiness and perfection are demanded. How can it be otherwise? Can God ignore or approve of any evil and sinful behavior being committed? The answer is no, and the reason is because of God's nature. He cannot relax His perfect standard of holiness and perfection.

If achieving perfection on our own is the only acceptable standard, then we should all just give up now. No matter who we are, no matter how spiritually mature we are, no one will ever be perfect by their own efforts and merit. However, we know God has taken this into consideration and has made a way for us to be acceptable to Him. God has made provisions for His children.

We see this reflected in the following Scriptures which put the previous Scriptures in context.

- **1 Peter 3:18**—For Christ died for sins once for all, the righteous for the unrighteous, to bring you to God.
- **Hebrews 10:12–14**—But when this priest [Jesus] had offered for all time one sacrifice for sins, he sat down at the right hand of God. Since that time he waits for his enemies to be made his footstool, because by one sacrifice he has made perfect forever those who are being made holy. [Us!]
- **1 John 2:1**—My dear children, I write this to you so that you will not sin. But if anybody does sin, we have one who speaks to the Father in our defense—Jesus Christ, the righteous one.
- **Romans 8:34**—Who is he that condemns? Christ Jesus who died—more than that, who was raised to life—is at the right hand of God and is also interceding for us."

Yes, God has provided a way! He had this in mind since before He made the heavens and the earth. The plan was in place before mankind was ever created (Eph. 1:3–4; Titus 1:2).

Jesus came to earth to be the bridge we need between us and God. The work Jesus did in sacrificing Himself on the cross of Calvary involving His death, burial, and resurrection was to impute forgiveness, righteousness, holiness, and perfection on to those of us who are born again. As we know, being born again reflects those of us who believe in Jesus, repent of our sins and turn toward God, accept Him as our Lord and Savior, and are buried with Him in baptism and raised from the dead to live a new life (Rom. 6:1–10). What Jesus did was a one-time sacrifice for all time. We are made holy through Jesus. His holiness is credited to us. Jesus comes to our defense when we make mistakes and sin. We remain in a reconciled state with God as we continue in the faith and maintain a relationship with Him.

Paul sums it up in **Colossians 1:21–23**:

> Once you were alienated from God and were enemies in your minds because of your evil behavior. But now he has reconciled you by Christ's physical body through death to present you holy in his sight, without blemish and free from accusation—if you continue in your faith, established and firm, and do not move from the hope held out in the gospel.

And so we see, God's provision for us to be holy and perfect is to remain faithful. Jesus does the rest.

In addition to the extremes of perfection, there are other passages of Scripture requiring us to do things that would be very difficult for us to do on our own, such as forgiving someone who has hurt us very deeply, for example, by viciously attacking and injuring our young child. It's like the scenario we see after the disciples were told by Jesus to forgive someone who sins against them seven times in a day, and then they respond, "Increase our faith" (Luke 17:5). I believe there are times when we can't do some very difficult things on our own without the help of the Holy Spirit.

As a professional Christian counselor, there were many times when I needed to encourage people who were struggling with self-esteem issues, perfectionistic thinking, and discouragement. There were many who felt they could never measure up to what was expected of them or needed from them for many reasons. There are many problematic conditions that could arise from these issues.

We need to realize we don't have to be perfect to be acceptable. We are just as valuable as any other person regardless of his or her situation or status. We are all made in the image of God, gloriously made. We need to focus on improving ourselves and not on trying to be like someone else or to change or control others (which we can't do anyway).

God Wants Us to Do Our Best

I believe God wants us to be the best we can be. I believe this is a pattern in Scripture when a level of commitment and dedication is required, such as loving God with all our hearts and fulfilling the golden rule found in Matthew 7:12. It is becoming clearer to me that God does not refer to quantity in what He asks of us in the Scriptures. It's not about how much we do or reaching a defined amount of something. God has no measuring stick or gauge He uses to judge us. It seems clear to me that He is concerned about quality, the efforts of our hearts. God does not set an exact amount for what He wants from us. This is because He wants us to pursue Him by continually seeking more and doing more out of our love for Him. God does not want us to think we've arrived at the goal and now can coast.

Being acceptable to God does not require total obedience or total anything. We should reject anyone who tries to impose that legalistic standard on us. We can't be perfect, and that is okay. We need to be faithful. We may need to be encouraged to do better or more, but don't let anyone place on you an impossible benchmark. For Christians, this is where grace plays an overriding role. Our perfection is credited to us through the work of Jesus.

So, let's keep going!

CHAPTER 2

Fruit Production

A Partnership Effort with God

"Those who live according to the flesh have their minds
set on what the flesh desires; but those who live in
accordance with the Spirit have their minds set on what
the Spirit desires."

—Romans 8:5

As I mentioned in the introduction of this book, critical thinking requires us to be able to deal with alternative viewpoints. Looking at different sides of an issue, doing research on challenging issues, and coming to a conclusion regarding one's own viewpoint is part of the process of deeper thinking. When researching a topic, we will often find writers who approach subjects from very different perspectives. This is especially true today in the realm of Christianity. This reality makes it much more complicated for everyone.

I will present some of the conflicting viewpoints people have expressed about how we produce fruit with the Holy Spirit and how we walk by the Spirit. There are many who believe in an extreme notion that it is only the Holy Spirit who produces the fruit mentioned in Galatians 5:22–23 with no involvement from ourselves. I will offer an alternative viewpoint. My aim in doing this is to correct the false notion just made and also make a convincing case for the viewpoint that God wants to have a unique partnership relationship with each of us.

What Some People Say

Immediately below, we will begin looking at several comments from various authors of books and articles on how they believe the Holy Spirit is working in people to help them produce the fruit of the Spirit mentioned in Galatians 5:22–23. They share the idea that God takes control of everything and apply this to the production of the fruit of the Spirit. I first assembled a much larger listing of comments but pared them down so as not to overkill the point here. This indicates how prevalent these ideas are out there. The following is how they expressed it:

- "Perhaps it would be best to begin by explaining what the fruit of the Spirit is not. It is not the result of any effort anyone can make. Not the effort to have faith or obey or to be loving and kind. The fruit of the Spirit has nothing directly to do with any exertion a believer can make."[23]
- "The fruit of the Spirit is produced by the Spirit, not by the Christian."[24]
- "It is only as we are filled with the Holy Spirit and under His control that His fruit is manifest and His will expressed..."[25]
- "This book is about producing the fruit of the Spirit, the very fruit that comes from God himself. We cannot produce it on our own."[26]
- "You cannot consistently display the fruit of the Spirit unless you have totally surrendered your life to Jesus Christ."[27]
- Regarding kindness: "Again, this is something which we must allow the Holy Spirit to do. Indeed, we do not have the capacity to do this in our own strength."[28]
- "The Holy Spirit controls the believer who yields to God and submits himself to God's word. When these conditions are met, the believer lives in the power of the Spirit and produces the fruit of the Spirit."[29]
- "These godly qualities are not something we can manufacture, take pride in, or claim to as self-generated. Rather, they are the work of God, and their source is God alone."[30]

This sampling of comments, although limited, does reflect the widespread views of many Christian groups, especially ones that currently dominate the internet as well as books written on the topic of the fruit of the

Spirit. Just because these groups dominate the internet does not mean their views represent a majority of people. What this tells us is that they spend a lot of time and money to be the ones found on internet searches. This is a result of what is known as "search engine optimization" (SEO), seeking to be the first ones found on internet searches. There are many Christians who would not share the views of these groups.

Contemplating the above statements can generate a lot of questions. One concern from common sense logic is that if it is indeed the Holy Spirit who produces all of the fruit of the Spirit, one would then conclude that all Christians would be highly successful in the fulfillment and expression of these qualities. That's because the Holy Spirit could only have perfect success if He was in control and the sole one responsible for producing the fruit. If God only gave people partial amounts of these qualities, wouldn't that show weakness and inability on the part of God? Why would God only give partial amounts of these qualities that are so important to the Christian life?

However, if believers fall short and don't display the fruit of the Spirit deeply and broadly, who then is to blame? If we contend and insist that the fruit is produced by the Holy Spirit alone, then the Holy Spirit would get all the blame when people fall short. Keep in mind that falling short in applying the fruit could involve mistreating people in offensive and hurtful ways. These results can come from being unkind, impatient, angry, argumentative, aggressive, insensitive, and so on. But this can't be. God does not make mistakes. God does not fall short in fulfilling His responsibilities. God would not mistreat people.

Now we know all Christians are not perfect and struggle with developing many of the nine qualities listed in Galatians 5:22–23. Because this is true, it must be because people have a large role in the production and implementation of these qualities. How could it be otherwise? The point I will be making regarding all of this is to highlight the partnership relationship we have with God, where we make every effort to develop these qualities, and the Holy Spirit helps us. Again, karpós represents two life streams at work at the same time, ours and God's.

So, if it is indeed the Holy Spirit who solely produces the fruit of the Spirit in Galatians 5, does this role of the Holy Spirit only relate to this one passage of Scripture? Would it relate to all spiritual matters? Would the Holy Spirit be the one to solely produce other godly qualities in our lives? If the Holy Spirit does it all, does that mean we do nothing? Can we produce anything?

To prepare for and get qualified to work in a variety of careers, such as business, engineering, philosophy, the medical profession's many careers, professional counseling, you name it, even religious jobs, one must go through a process of devoted study to learn and apply the material. How is attaining biblical qualities, such as the fruit of the Spirit, any different? Developing these qualities in our lives involves study, observing, learning, testing, valuing, making mistakes, re-evaluating, and practice. What process of learning and developing skills and abilities does not take the effort of our minds and our self-control? Why does the Bible speak often about attaining knowledge, understanding, and maturity? After all, what does maturity mean?

If the Holy Spirit does it all, then we have nothing to do with it. Why then does the Bible talk so often about qualities we must have (develop) to be godly? Why have appeals for us to do certain things in Scripture if we have no role in doing what we are told to do? Why preach on these topics, have Bible studies, and have other learning opportunities if it is the Holy Spirit who does (produces) it all on His own?

We hear some pastors and Christian leaders say we must completely surrender to God. How many of us even know what "complete surrender" to God means? Who can say they do anything totally or completely?

I believe we would all agree that God, our Creator, is all powerful. He has the right to set up the way the world operates and how He would structure the relationship He chooses to have with mankind. God has the choice to reveal to mankind as much as He wants to about His nature and attributes. It is these kinds of revelations in the Scriptures that provide the framework for understanding how God interacts with us.

Is There Virtue to Surrendering Control?

There are many well-meaning believers who try to express the notion of God controlling us in positive terms. Many people are more than willing to accept the notion that they are controlled by the Holy Spirit. They see it as being uniquely spiritual to allow the Holy Spirit to take control. Many interpret the metaphor "filled with the Spirit" to mean the time in which the Spirit takes control. They proudly proclaim that complete surrender is a sign of amazing obedience to Christ. They say we cannot experience the glory of God's power without totally yielding to Him. They claim the greatest happiness and the pathway to experiencing godly power is found by letting the Holy Spirit indwell the lives of believers in a controlling fashion.

Dr. Bill Bright, co-founder of the Campus Crusade for Christ, is one such person who firmly believes this is how the Holy Spirit works in people's lives. After quoting a Scripture of Jesus saying to the apostles that they will do even greater things than He has done (John 14:12), he applied that passage to mean the following today.

> Obviously, you cannot, in your own energy, accomplish these great works. It is Christ himself—living within you in all of his resurrection power, walking around in your body, thinking with your mind, loving with your heart, speaking with your lips—who will empower you with the Holy Spirit to do these great works. It is not your wisdom, your eloquence, your logic, your good personality, or your persuasiveness which brings people to our Savior. It is the Son of Man, who came to seek and to save the lost, who sent His Holy Spirit to fill and empower you. [31]

This seems to be a pretty radical way of imagining how the Holy Spirit operates in our lives. How many of us can say we've experienced what Dr. Bright describes above? How would one know this for certain?

My question is, are we really expected to believe that each of us have no capability or responsibility when it comes to developing love, joy, peace, patience, and the other qualities included in the fruit of the Spirit passage? Are we just to surrender to God and expect Him to do all of this for us?

If the Holy Spirit produces all of the fruit, then the logical assumption is that we are not producing any of the fruit. In this scenario, the fruit would not be coming from any of our efforts. The fruit would not be coming from our heart, our minds, our strength, or our abilities. How does Jesus speak with our lips and think with our minds anyway? Where does Jesus mention anything about this process? Again, if the fruit is not coming from our efforts, how can we claim any responsibility for fulfilling what we are told to do in the Scriptures and be accountable for our efforts?

As an example of what I am trying to explain, what do parents spend a great deal of time on when their children are very young? They all try to teach them how to understand concepts, think for themselves, develop self-control, and become properly socialized. Parenting is all about equipping our children to be self-sufficient human beings, to be able to handle their lives on their own. In fact, all children long to be able to learn new things and do things on their own. Do these concepts only apply when they are young or before they take the steps to be born again? Do people stop using their brains when they become Christians and then just let the Holy Spirit control them? No parent would want their children to be dependent on them for how to live every detail of the lives, for all of their lives. I believe God would also not want us to be totally dependent on Him for everything for the rest of our lives after we are born again. On the contrary, He takes delight in how we glorify Him through our godly efforts and actions on the road to becoming spiritually mature. Expecting God to take control of all things in our lives does not fit the scriptural description of this godly pattern. It fails to meet the simple basics of godly logic.

When God tells us and expects us to do things, He wants us to use our skills and abilities to do them. He wants us to do our best. When is it appropriate to not give our best effort? The Scriptures tell us that the Holy Spirit is present to help us but not to be our substitute. If we don't exert the effort to the best of our abilities to produce the fruit of the Spirit and establish other spiritual qualities, then it's like we are refusing to obey the Scriptures. If we are not actively involved, it is like we are not trying, and it can appear we don't care.

As a Christian professional counselor, I've worked with people to help them deal with their personal issues, family issues, and marital issues. Counseling can be very helpful to both believers and unbelievers as they deal with past scars that have come from the impact of being in dysfunctional families as well as receiving mistreatment in many other ways. We can teach on forgiveness and help facilitate the process of letting go of resentments so they can be free to love again. We help people deal with problems with anger, insecurities, and self-esteem. Our counseling does not tell them to just totally and completely surrender to the Holy Spirit and let God handle all their issues. Our counseling is not to encourage them to get out of the way and just let God deal solely with their situations. We encourage prayer and following Scripture, but we don't advise them to abandon their efforts and expect God to handle it all. Counselors can only help people who want to be helped and are willing to cooperate in the therapeutic process.

Most of us clearly understand we are responsible for our own choices and behavior. We know we are given commands and appeals for action all throughout Scripture. It is up to us to obey God's Word. It is up to us to develop godly character and qualities. We have a lot of responsibility in all of this.

One of our great blessings is that we do have the Holy Spirit residing inside us to help us but not in a way to control and take over for us. I contend there are more biblically accurate concepts to follow than being deceived to believe that God wants to control us. It's a false argument to say that either God does it all and we just need to get out of the way or we do it all and God needs to get out of the way. Neither of these options is the scriptural way.

The way to a meaningful, purposeful, and authentic relationship with God is to engage earnestly in the partnership relationship we have with Him. It is us functioning in conjunction with God. This is the way God designed it from the very beginning. Consider the responsibilities God gave to Adam and Eve. God delights in seeing the people He created doing wonderful things. As Christians, we should all base our actions and expectations on what the applicable Scriptures say—the whole of Scriptures—not just picking and choosing selected verses here or there while ignoring other verses or using paraphrased versions of the Bible to try to prove our point or defend our doctrine.

Let's keep this in mind as we consider how we do what we can to have the qualities of the fruit of the Spirit and as we seek help from the Holy Spirit in this endeavor and in our lives as a whole.

Does God Really Want to Be in Control of Everything?

In my personal studies, I've learned how the term "God is in control" comes out of one's personal understanding of the "sovereignty of God." This debate over the sovereignty of God and the free will of man has been going on for centuries. There are primarily two camps in this debate. One is made up of those who firmly believe that God takes control of everything that happens. The other is made up of those who firmly believe that God does not want to control everything and has given mankind the power to make independent free will decisions as we live in partnership with Him.

Both groups feel very strongly about their positions. Both groups have their reasons for what they believe and why. Both believe that the Bible clearly supports their viewpoint. There are scholarly people on both sides. I've seen many who believe that God is in control of everything act as if this idea is not even in dispute. Well, that is certainly not so.

Having studied this issue for a long time and fairly deeply, I have come to agree with many others that free will believers clearly have the best arguments that are aligned with the character of God and the clear teaching of Scripture. One prominent pastor expressed his sentiments about the mistaken notion that God is in control of everything like this: "I believe this is the worst doctrine in the church today."[32] He was speaking about the Christian community as a whole. A large number of other church leaders would echo his sentiment.

Many of those who reject the notion that God is in control of everything will point out that the definition of the sovereignty of God does not have to be understood as God being in control of everything for Him to be sovereign.

From one perspective, we can look at the *Webster's Dictionary* to see how it defines the word "sovereign." It says: (1) above or superior to all others; chief; greatest; supreme, (2) supreme in power, rank or authority, (3) of or holding the position of ruler; royal; reigning, and (4) independent of all others. [33] Where do we see the notion of "control" here? We don't.

Many biblical scholars will say the word "sovereign" is not even in the Bible. However, it depends on the version of the Bible one is reading. The word "sovereign" is mentioned over 200 times in the New International Version (NIV). In other versions, it is not even mentioned once. The Greek word used for sovereign is **despotés** (pronounced des-pot'-ace), which describes an authority figure, a master, who exercises complete jurisdiction and unrestrained power. [34]

Over the years, some church leaders have given a new definition to the word "sovereign" to mean that God is in control of everything in order to correspond to their church doctrines. Many have their own written position statements for this. It is most likely that this redefining is the reason why this notion seems to be spreading so quickly and broadly. See below a definition of God's sovereignty by one Calvinist group:

> God's sovereignty is defined as His complete and total independent control over every creature, event, and circumstance at every moment in history. Subject to none, influenced by none, absolutely independent, God does what He pleases, only as He pleases, always as He pleases. God is in complete control of every molecule in the universe at every moment, and everything that happens is either caused or allowed by Him for His own perfect purposes. [35]

Since there are no Scriptures that specifically define God's sovereignty, it seems pretty bold to put such an explicit definition like this out there as being true and certain. Again, one will not find a definition like this in the Scriptures.

What we really need to do is to look for Scriptures that reflect God's greatness, His power, and His sovereignty. See the following for some of these.

- In the beginning God... (Gen. 1:1) Before there was anything else, there was God.
- God created the heavens and the earth (Gen. 1:1).
- He is called the Alpha and Omega—the beginning and the end (Rev. 22:13).
- He alone is immortal (1 Tim. 6:16).
- He is before all things, and in him all things hold together (Col. 1. 17).
- There is "one God and Father of all, who is over all and through all and in all" (Eph. 4:6).
- God is omniscient (knows all things)—(Ps. 147:5; Isa. 46:10; Heb. 4:13; Rom. 11:33).
- God can do all things (omnipotent—all powerful).
  o God created everything.
  o God does miracles.
  o God does whatever pleases him (Ps. 135:6).
  o Nothing is impossible with God (Luke 1:37 and Matt. 19:26).
    ▪ Regarding the notion that nothing is impossible with God, God can do whatever is possible to do. He won't act incongruent to his nature and attributes. He can't lie, He doesn't change (immutable), He won't make a mistake, He won't make a square a circle, and He won't make a triangle with two sides.
- There is no one else like God (Isa. 46:9–11).

These Scriptures don't have to collectively mean that sovereignty is defined as total control of everything.

Those who firmly believe God is in control of everything use the following Scriptures, and others, to support their view. The following comes from the book by Christopher Ash (a Calvinist) entitled, *Where Was God*

When That Happened: and Other Questions about God's Goodness, Power and the Way He Works in the World. [36]

- God controls everything: Psalm115:3; Ephesians 1:11; Daniel 4:35.
- God is utterly and completely in control. No restrictions and no limitations: Psalm 104:14; Matthew 5:45; Psalm 148:8; Psalm 104:21, 27.
- God controls natural processes and the weather: Psalm 104:14; Matthew 5:45; Psalm 148:8.
- God controls human beings: Proverbs 21:1; Ezra 6:22; Isaiah 44:28; 45:1.
- God decrees what we then freely decide: Acts 17:26.
- God is in control of every place: Psalm 139:8.
- God controls random events: Proverbs 16:33; 21:31.
- God controls the future: Acts 1:7; 2 Peter 3:8.
- God controls evil: Isaiah 45:7.

Even though Mr. Ash and other similar-minded people like to firmly assert that God is in control of everything, there is not one passage of Scripture provided that explicitly and clearly says this. If you will look closely at each of the Scriptures he uses above to make his case, you can see how those passages can reasonably be interpreted in other ways.

The nagging question remains, "Where in the Scriptures is the concept that God is taking control of everything clearly explained to us?" If God does want to control everything, this concept would be huge for how we understand our experiences in life and how God would be connected to them. This would be a very important topic for us to understand. Because of this, one would expect the Scriptures to plainly, frequently, and unambiguously speak to this. If true, a concept like this would not be left to such uncertainty, confusion, and doubt.

Consider this: why are there many Scriptures repeatedly referring to certain topics that are not as impactful as the notion of God being in control of everything? We see some concepts discussed over and over again, such as asking us to show compassion, kindness, gentleness, self-control, humility, and so on. Why don't we see Scriptures explaining that God is in control over and over again? Why is it we don't even see one single passage of Scripture explicitly saying this?

Yes, we see God acting mightily in Scripture to bring about His plan and will in both the Old and New Testaments. He uses great men and women of faith to affect the circumstances needed at the given time. The great people of faith are often common people in the community. Consider the apostles. However, this does not have to mean that God works by being in control of everything for all people. Yes, God does at times step in and interrupt the lives of people He wants to forward His purposes (such as Abraham and the apostles), but that does not mean He does this in a controlling fashion.

Consider the great abilities God has given to mankind. We know mankind has been created in God's image. People have a brain and can make decisions on what to do. We know that much of what people decide to do is influenced by the heart of the person. Therefore, the question arises, "Does God then control the mind and heart of people?" Are we to assume that God controls all of our thoughts and decisions? Is this even minutely alluded to in the Scriptures? Are we to believe that God controls us, even if we don't give Him permission to do so? Can we even fathom how this can happen? Again, if this is true, then what responsibility do we have for any of our actions if God is controlling them? Also, in that scenario, where would accountability for our actions be directed?

Yes, many people believe that God is in control and is the one who puts sickness and disease in their lives so that He can work something for good in their lives. If they truly believe this, why would they go to the doctor or take any medicine? According to their views, wouldn't that be resisting God's plans? Shouldn't they just let the sickness run its course and thereby get the full benefit of God's purpose in this? Now, except for just a few small religious movements, I don't know of anyone who would advocate for this. It seems clearly absurd. It is even more absurd to believe that God is the one behind the tragedy of all sicknesses and diseases that occur over time. However, if the concept of God being in control is true, it would force us to accept this idea.

Control is not one of the themes we see in the Scriptures. What we see are themes relating to the responsibility for us to have godly character, attitudes, and behaviors. We don't find Jesus communicating the message of control.

Free Will Is Important

The idea of mankind having independent free will is a concept that runs throughout the Scriptures and must be understood in light of the sovereignty of God. We understand the role of free will by deduction, not direct pronouncement. The Scriptures don't use the phrase "free will" outright. However, we see free will playing a clear role in the major stories involving the experiences of key biblical figures as they were regularly faced with having to make distinct choices. We see the necessity of free will when authority figures in the Scriptures give us commands, encouragements, admonitions, and standards to live by as we follow Christ.

God gives people a moral responsibility that can only be fulfilled with free choice. Free will reflects that we have control over ourselves. Without free will, we would not be responsible or accountable for our actions. Without free will, we could not freely love God. Freedom is a condition of love. We are to love God with all our heart. This can't come from being forced to do it. God does not force anyone to love Him or accept His love. Force cannot produce love. True love can only come voluntarily from the heart.

Nowhere does the Bible state that man has no power to make genuine choices, moral or otherwise. In fact, the opposite is the case. Nowhere in the Scriptures does God have a sense of not being sovereign and all-powerful even though He created man with free will. As we noted by looking at the definition of sovereignty, God can be sovereign without controlling everything.

God appeals to human reasoning all the time. This underscores the assumption that people have free will. God is a God of logic and reason. To get us to do things, He uses explanation and persuasion, not power and control. The command central for regulating the thoughts and behaviors of human beings is our mind. It does not occur from an external force controlling us.

It can be argued that making humans with free will is God's most marvelous and consequential accomplishment. It is, indeed, the gift that makes possible every other gift from God. Without the power to choose, man could not consciously receive any gift from God. We are told that salvation is a gift (Eph. 2:8). By its very nature, a gift must be received by an act of the will. If a gift is forced upon the recipient, then it is not a gift.

The Need to Be Seekers of the Truth

It seems obvious that few people who are firmly entrenched in their doctrinal positions will change their views. However, if we have disagreements, we should be able to discuss these with love, respect, gentleness, and self-control. Unfortunately, many times this is not the case.

We all would say we need to stand on the truth. There are few things more important than truth. However, we know truth may not be easy to find at times. We all must be sincere seekers of the truth. As the Scriptures say, we must be cautious about false teachers (Matt. 7:15; 2 Pet. 2:1–2; Rom. 16:17; Eph. 5:11; 1 John 4:16; 1 Tim. 1:10–11).

The question is, whose responsibility is it to find the truth? Do we let others dominate and control our thinking, and we just go along? Or, should we go to greater lengths personally to seek and find the truth? We must realize that differing views can't all be true. We should carefully examine differing ideas as we make our own decisions about what is true or not.

What the Scriptures Say about the Holy Spirit

The Bible certainly has much to say about the role of the Holy Spirit. The focus of this section will be to provide evidence that the Holy Spirit is not about controlling believers. This section will not attempt to be an exhaustive study on the Holy Spirit. Trying to explain fully how the Holy Spirit is manifested through us today is beyond the scope of this book.

We know the Holy Spirit is not an "it." The Holy Spirit is the third person in the Godhead: God the Father, Jesus the Son, and the Holy Spirit, our advocate. The Holy Spirit, therefore, is to be understood in the context of how we understand God and Jesus. The Holy Spirit has all the attributes of God and Jesus, which means the Holy Spirit cannot be fully understood, controlled, or manipulated.

As part of the Godhead, some have called the Holy Spirit the "Executor" of the Trinity—the one who carries out God's work in our world. It is safe to say that the work of the Holy Spirit is always in accordance with the purposes of God. Therefore, when we come across the Holy Spirit in the Bible, we find God in action.

Although Jesus alluded to the Holy Spirit a few times previously in the gospel of John (John 7:37–39), Jesus more fully introduces the Holy Spirit to His disciples nearing the time of His crucifixion in what some call the "final discourse" Jesus has with His apostles in chapters 13–16. We read in **John 14:15–17**:

> If you love me, keep my commands. And I will ask the Father, and he will give you another advocate to help you and be with you forever—the Spirit of truth. The world cannot accept him, because it neither sees him nor knows him. But you know him, for he lives with you and will be in you.

The Greek word for "advocate" in the above Scripture is "**parakletos**" (pronounced par-ak'-lay-tos).[37] The definition of this word encompasses advocate, intercessor, comforter, and helper. The image here is of a legal advocate who understands the situation well and makes the right judgment calls.

Jesus then tells His apostles the following in **John 14:26**:

> But the Counselor, the Holy Spirit, whom the Father will send in my name, will teach you all things and will remind you of everything I have said to you.

The apostles will be equipped to carry on the work of Jesus because the Holy Spirit will be with them and provide incredible and miraculous support to their efforts.

Jesus spoke of the work of the Holy Spirit in **John 16:7–15**:

> But very truly I tell you, it is for your good that I am going away. Unless I go away, the Advocate will not come to you; but if I go, I will send him to you. When he comes, he will convict the world of guilt regarding sin and righteousness and judgment: in regard to sin, because people do not believe in me; in regard to righteousness, because I am going to the Father, where you can see me no longer; and in regard to judgment, because the prince of this world now stands condemned.
>
> I have much more to say to you, more than you can now bear. But when he, the Spirit of truth, comes, he will guide you into all the truth. He will not speak on his own; he will

speak only what he hears, and he will tell you what is yet to come. He will glorify me because it is from me that he will receive what he will make known to you. All that belongs to the Father is mine. That is why I said the Spirit will receive from me what he will make known to you.

Here again Jesus calls the Holy Spirit "the Advocate." Other translations say, "the helper" or "counselor." Here Jesus talks about the impact the Spirit will have on the "world," what we could also refer to as "unbelievers." The Holy Spirit works in the lives of unbelievers by convicting them of sin, righteousness, and judgment (John 16:8). Some say that this is the only work that the Holy Spirit does in the life of the unbeliever. Jesus then tells His apostles that the Spirit will guide them into all the truth (John 16:13). He goes on to say that He will give the Holy Spirit directions for what the Holy Spirit is to communicate to them (John 16:14). The work of the Holy Spirit is certainly incredibly significant to the apostles. Jesus tells them that it is for their good that He is going away so that the Holy Spirit can come to be with them.

What we know is to come is great power given to the apostles as they have an incredible task ahead of them to evangelize an unchristian world.

Being Filled with the Holy Spirit

We read in the Scriptures where we are to be "filled with the Spirit." However, I don't think it is ever explained in the Scriptures what being filled with the Spirit means. We can see that the phrase "filled with the Holy Spirit" is a metaphor as the word "filled" is symbolic language. Many questions arise regarding this concept:

- How do we know when we are filled with the Holy Spirit?
- How do we know when we are not filled with the Holy Spirit?
- What will we see happen when we are filled with the Holy Spirit?
- How is being filled with the Holy Spirit different than when we are not filled with the Holy Spirit, if this is the case?
- Are we filled with the Spirit at all times or only part of the time?
- What can we know about what "filled" means, explicitly and with certainty?
- How do we even find answers to these questions?

In **Ephesians 5:18**, the apostle Paul says:

> Do not get drunk on wine, which leads to debauchery.
> Instead, be filled with the Spirit.

The Greek word for "filled" is **pléroó** (pronounced play-ro'-o) and means "being made full, complete, full in quantity."[38] From this, we must not get a sense in which being filled with the Holy Spirit indicates that some have only received gradations or parts of the Holy Spirit and not all of the Holy Spirit. When we receive the Holy Spirit, we get all of the Holy Spirit. How can we say otherwise?

From the passages in which the phrase "filled with the Holy Spirit" is used, we may get some idea what this means based on what is said in association with the phrase. Consider the following.

We read a passage of Scripture about being filled with the Spirit in **Acts 4:31**:

> After they prayed, the place where they were meeting was shaken. And they were all filled with the Holy Spirit and spoke the word of God boldly.

So, the apostles spoke the Word of God boldly after being filled with the Holy Spirit. It would certainly be reasonable to consider that this is how the Holy Spirit was manifested in them when they were filled with the Holy Spirit.

Great Power at Work

We read in the Scriptures in Acts 1:1–2 about the teaching and instructions Jesus gave to the apostles up until the eve of His crucifixion. In **Acts 1:8**, before Jesus ascended into heaven, He tells His apostles the following:

> But you will receive power when the Holy Spirit comes on you; and you will be my witnesses in Jerusalem, and in all Judea and Samaria, and to the ends of the earth.

Here Jesus tells them that the power of the Holy Spirit will enable them to testify to the world about Christ.

The apostle Paul talks about the power of the Holy Spirit in **Ephesians 3:14–21**:

> For this reason I kneel before the Father, from whom every family in heaven and on earth derives its name. I pray that out of his glorious riches he may strengthen you with power through his Spirit in your inner being, so that Christ may dwell in your hearts through faith. And I pray that you, being rooted and established in love, may have power, together with all the Lord's holy people, to grasp how wide and long and high and deep is the love of Christ, and to know this love that surpasses knowledge—that you may be filled to the measure of all the fullness of God.
>
> Now to him who is able to do immeasurably more than all we ask or imagine, according to his power that is at work within us, to him be glory in the church and in Christ Jesus throughout all generations, forever and ever! Amen.

This is one of the most descriptive passages of Scripture relating to the power we receive from the Holy Spirit. The results mentioned are: (1) so that Christ may dwell in our hearts through faith, (2) that we will be able to grasp how extensive is the love of Christ, (3) that we may be filled to the measure of all the fullness of God, and (4) this power that is at work within us is imaginable and immeasurable. This all relates to the tremendous influence and power the Holy Spirit has within us. This is all the information we are given with this passage. There are no explanations as to what these ideas mean and how specifically the Holy Spirit is manifested in the lives of believers.

Metaphors are often used when describing what the Holy Spirit does for us. We understand that everyone has the freedom to interpret a metaphor any way they want.

Again, we are told in the Scriptures to:

- Be **led** by the Holy Spirit (Rom. 8:11–14; Gal. 5:18);
- **Walk** by the Holy Spirit (Gal. 5:16, 25);
- Be **filled** with the Holy Spirit (Eph. 5:18);
- The Spirit **guides** us into all the truth... (John 16:13); and

- The Spirit is described as an **advocate, helper, counselor...** (John 16:7).

Do any of the above passages give us the explicit idea that the Holy Spirit controls us? There are no Scriptures that specifically or implicitly say that the Holy Spirit controls us. Again, I believe this is because God does not want to control but persuade. How can one have a healthy relationship if one is being controlled? Control usually requires coercion, and that is not God's way. It's the nature of God to woo, not overwhelm.[39]

Many realize that the idea of God being in control and controlling us is heard very frequently in the Christian community in all kinds of faith/church backgrounds. We hear many songs of contemporary Christian music with lyrics affirming such ideas. It's all around us. However, that does not make it true.

Some may say that we can invite God to come into our lives and control us. The idea here is that we can give permission to God to control us. It does not have to mean God forces himself upon us. Now, would that be a standing invite? Would it never change? Even if we invite God to do something, if it is not His way, He won't anyway. We should not expect God to do things unless the Scriptures are clear God does those things.

One of the most popular Scriptures about the work of the Holy Spirit is found in Romans 8. Here the apostle Paul tells us to set our minds on the Spirit. I believe this is stated in terms of how we embrace and engage the power of the Holy Spirit.

Romans 8:5–8 (NASB):

> For those who are according to the flesh set their minds on the things of the flesh, but those who are according to the Spirit, the things of the Spirit. For the mind set on the flesh is death, but the mind set on the Spirit is life and peace, because the mind set on the flesh is hostile toward God; for it does not subject itself to the law of God, for it is not even able to do so, and those who are in the flesh cannot please God.

In an older version of the NIV for verse 6, it says, "The mind of the sinful man is death, but the mind controlled by the Spirit is life..." Instead of using "controlled by the Spirit," the better rendering of this passage is "set on the Spirit." Actually, in the NIV, the word "controlled" is used three times in verses 6, 8, and 9 of chapter 8. However, the word "controlled" here does not fit with the Greek word rendering of what is being said here. Other versions do not use the word "controlled." Again, the work of the Holy Spirit will not bypass our brains. The Holy Spirit will enlighten our minds.

General Overview on the Holy Spirit

Again, as I understand it, there are no Scriptures that speak of the Holy Spirit controlling us. The Scriptures talk of the Holy Spirit indwelling believers. The Holy Spirit does not operate in us without our permission and participation. The Holy Spirit does not force us to surrender our will or abilities to make free choices in order to have the Holy Spirit's guidance. That is not the Holy Spirit's way. God wants a partnership with us where we use our abilities and He helps us. That is how God made us. When did it change? It didn't. God expects much from us.

No, God did not create us to be controlled by Him. He is not a dictator or puppeteer. The Holy Spirit instructs but does not insist. The Holy Spirit teaches but does not put people under a spell. The Holy Spirit empowers but does not overpower. The Holy Spirit does not dominate our minds. Again, the Holy Spirit is our helper, not our controller.

Having discussions about boundaries of the Holy Spirit is needed because of misconceptions associated with the role of the Holy Spirit. What, hopefully, we all can agree on is that we want to take advantage of all that the Holy Spirit can do for us. No one wants to limit or miss out on the power we can receive from the Holy Spirit. My perspective on this is, as Christians, we do our best in following Jesus and living godly lives. We pray and ask God for strength and then expect the Holy Spirit to give us whatever power and strength He chooses to give us. We then accept the outcome.

I know some people ask for a greater portion of the Holy Spirit. However, I don't think we should ask for "more" of the Holy Spirit. We are filled with the Holy Spirit at the point when we receive the Holy Spirit. We don't just receive a portion of the Holy Spirit, whatever that might mean. We access the Spirit by focusing our minds on what the Holy Spirit desires (Rom. 8:5–8). We focus our minds on godly and spiritual things.

Some preachers have said that we need to plug into the power of the Holy Spirit. This is a metaphor, but I don't see how it is a correct one. Do

30

we plug into something we already have? The Holy Spirit is within us. He knows who we are and what we need. If we are living godly lives, we will receive the strength, guidance, and help God wants to give us. We need to remember what the Holy Spirit does for one person may be different for another. I don't find a formula in the Scriptures revealing the exact process of how the Holy Spirit operates for all of us in all circumstances other than what I've been saying in this section.

It would seem obvious that some Christians can turn away from God and put their focus in other places, such as things of this world. This can't be good for expecting the Holy Spirit to help us.

Our Partnership Relationship with God

Working together with God is a common theme throughout the Bible. Being made in the likeness of God implies God made us with great skills and abilities. God has elected to work in partnership with us. He started doing this with Adam and Eve. We all know how God has chosen to work through prophets, priests, apostles, and those we can call the giants of the faith mentioned throughout the Scriptures. God needs His people, "saints" as Christians are sometimes called, to cooperate with Him, and we certainly need God.

Now some may say that God does not need anyone. If that is the case, we are irrelevant. Why then would God have created us? After the creation, the great accomplishments of God we see throughout the Scriptures have involved people. All of this points to the special relationship we have with God. I like to call this relationship an interdependent type of relationship. Yes, there is no doubt that we need God more than He needs us, but that is not the point. God values us and loves us dearly. We should value and love ourselves greatly because of this.

This partnership is predicated upon the reality that we have a close and trusting relationship with God. The partnership we have with God reflects how God entrusts us to do things using our intellectual and physical abilities, personalities, strengths, interests, and talents as well as our experiences, training, and education and background. We use these to partner with Him to provide for our needs and the needs of others to accomplish His purposes. The careers we pursue are often based on our personalities, interests, and talents. God has created us to have great abilities. To look down upon the abilities of human beings is really a slam on God as if He couldn't create mankind with wonderful enduring qualities and abilities. Yes, we know He did and He wants us to use these as we journey together with Him through life.

I've had a clinical license in social work for over thirty years before voluntarily surrendering this with retirement. I first obtained my master's of science in social work degree (MSSW), and after a few years, underwent clinical supervision while providing psychotherapy. I then passed the state exam for the clinical license. I've also participated in many hours of continuing education over the course of my career and have done a great deal of reading and studying to learn about many issues people struggle with in their lives. I became very skilled at doing the work I was doing.

I remember the time I spoke to a counseling colleague who is also a Christian. He told me that he prayed before each session, asking God to get him out of the way so that the Holy Spirit would lead the counseling session. This is a prime example of what I disagree with, even as well-meaning Christians seek to be as spiritual as they can be.

As a partner with God, I don't believe God uses me by stripping away all my skills, abilities, knowledge, and experience to replace me, so to speak, by stepping in to take over in the counseling sessions. I believe God wants me to use my skills, abilities, training, and experience to help people to the best of my abilities. I believe God is with me in the sessions.

I think of the apostle Paul and his personality and abilities. Paul briefly lists the reasons he can have confidence in the flesh in Philippians 3:4–7. Paul had demonstrated great strength of character and leadership qualities, although misguided, as he went about defending his Jewish faith by persecuting Christians in compliance with the high priest's wishes. This occurred before his conversion as explained in Acts chapter 9. I believe God chose Paul precisely because he was such a strong, accomplished, and zealous person with great potential to take on the role God wanted him to play.

God did not want to strip those positive qualities away from Paul. He wanted to use those abilities for His purposes. Yes, we read where Paul does say that God had given him the gift of His grace through the working of His power to do the things God wanted him to do (Eph. 3:7). God knew he was the right person at the right time for the ministry God had in store for him.

God put Paul in the position He did to be able to use Paul's personal qualities for accomplishing God's work. God did not look for an insecure, emotionally damaged, weak person for the ministry He had in store for Paul. Similarly, I firmly believe God does not want to erase our personalities, strengths, and life experiences just for Him to come into our lives and take over for us.

Conclusion

God has given each human being the gift of free will. We need to exercise this free will at all times. We can expect the Holy Spirit to complement our efforts. We should always give our best efforts in all we do in our journey with God.

We learn a lot from experience. If we do well or make some mistakes, all of this can be used by God to help us for the future. As we seek to do what is right and as we seek to be led by God's Spirit, we may not know how God is helping and leading us. Must we expect or rely on a physical or mental sign or a clear word from God or some kind of confirmation? As believers, we just need to know God is with us even if we don't have a sign. Actually, we don't need a sign. We should not expect a sign. We don't have to have full understanding. We have a promise. We just need to trust that God is with us at all times. Our faith is what pleases God.

I hope you see how this has been a powerful chapter filled with important concepts to consider. It does challenge some common views held onto tightly by many people. I pray you let the Scriptures speak to you and not just the words of human beings with a biased perspective.

CHAPTER 3

Love

Our Highest Priority

God is love. Whoever lives in love lives in God, and
God in him.

—1 John 4:16

Be imitators of God, therefore, as dearly loved children
and live a life of love...

—Ephesians 5:1

The only thing that matters is faith expressing itself
through Love.

—Galatians 5:6

We now come to love, the first fruit of the Spirit in Galatians 5:22–23. This
is a small word with tremendous meaning and implication for our lives.
Love is one of the most important and broadly discussed topics in the New
Testament. It is one of the most complex topics in all of Scripture. Love is
the most important topic by far aside from God, Jesus, and the Holy Spirit.
That is why we must dig deep into many of its dimensions.

Many may say love is easy, but in reality, its demands and obligations
can be quite challenging. The pursuit to love as we should is a never-ending
quest. We never achieve the limitless demands of love. It's a lifelong continual

endeavor. It should always be in our consciousness. The motivating power of love should compel us to explore its outer limits and discover its vastness. True love always wants more. True love is never satisfied with a minimal or mediocre experience. True love never asks, "What is the least I can do to get by?"

As we know, the English language uses just one word for love, which makes it more difficult to understand its many dimensions. In the Greek language, the language of the New Testament, there are several different words for love used with each having its separate and distinct meaning. The four most prominent are: (1) agape (the deepest, purest kind of love, focused on the needs of others), (2) phileo/philia (friendship, fondness, and personal affection), (3) storge (family affection), and (4) eros (romantic and sexual love). The kind of love we are commanded to have in the Scriptures is ***agape***. This will be our focus. We'll look deeper into what this means shortly.

Why Is Love so Important?

The word love is mentioned 551 times in the New International Version of the Bible and 538 times in the New Revised Standard Version. These numbers only tell a small portion of the story.[40]

There are many Scriptures that elevate love above all the virtues and godly qualities we are to have in our lives (1 Cor. 13; Matt. 22:37–40). Loving God and others, the first and second greatest commandments, represents the highest of devotion (Luke 10:27–28). If anything can be said to be primary, central, and essential to being a Christian and becoming more like Jesus, it is love. Love is the most important godly attribute. Love is the predominant quality by which a Christian should be known. Love is always relevant. Love has the power to touch and influence everything. Love is our primary Christian duty. It is above all else in value.

As we've noticed already, the Bible is all about love. Since love is indirectly communicated using a variety of words, we can then appreciate how prevalently this topic is expressed throughout the Scriptures. This includes words and concepts representing the meaning of love, such as compassion, kindness, mercy, patience, goodness, forgiveness, reconciliation, gentleness, repentance, humility, honor, generosity, encouragement, and many others. Even when words are not being used, the agape kind of love is the motivation behind the instructions, commands, and major stories in the Scriptures, including the actions of Jesus and the apostles. Yes, the Bible at its core is a message of love.

Even though the above is true, the reason why comes from God. Love is of preeminent importance because God, our Creator, is love. We can infer that love is God's greatest attribute for many reasons. One is because it is related to the greatest commandment He gives mankind (Matt. 22:37–40). This is where we are commanded to love God and others. God wants us to be like Him in this way. God also knows what is best for us. We are made with the need to have love, receive love, and give love. This is embedded deeply into our human nature. It is part of the way God has gloriously designed us.

Love relates to a major reason why God made humans in the first place. Our purpose in life is aligned with how God designed us as human beings. Following the way of love places us in this alignment. Love always leads to the right things to do. How important it is, then, to know the way of love (Eph. 5:2).

Love Permeates the Fruit of the Spirit

We see that love is the first quality or character trait mentioned in the listing of the fruit of the Spirit in Galatians 5:22–23. It seems obvious that this is due to the overriding importance of love and its relationship to the other eight qualities mentioned. Each of the other eight qualities can be seen as manifestations of love. Therefore, it also seems clear that love is the overriding motive in the expression of each of them. A lack in the amount of each of the qualities in our lives is a sign of a lack of love. It can be said that love is the common thread that binds all of these qualities together.

After listing qualities that include several from the Galatians passage, Paul says in Colossians 3:14 that love binds all of the qualities together in perfect unity. These qualities are not in total isolation. They are connected to each other by love. Without love, none of the qualities could be rightly manifested.

Another way of saying this is to acknowledge that all of the qualities of the fruit are qualities of God's character. It is this insight that reveals why love ties and binds all of the fruit together in unity.

The Sequence of This Chapter

There are five major aspects we need to understand and pursue as we address the topic of love. They are: (1) God is love; (2) God's love for us; (3) our love for God; (4) loving our neighbors as ourselves; and (5) loving others as Christ has loved us. They are all connected. This is what we will unpack in the remainder of this chapter as we deal with the breadth of this concept.

1. God Is Love

We are told in 1 John 4:8 that God is love. The Greek word used for love in that passage of Scripture is "agape." The agape way to love is a defining characteristic of God. Love starts with God. It's not merely that God loves others. God's love is the primary characteristic and motivation for everything. He can't do otherwise. If we want to be like God, we must seek to have hearts and minds, which are oriented to agape and, indeed, full of agape. We must be constant transmitters of agape.

We love because He first loved us (1 John 4:19). This is a pattern in the Scriptures. God does things first and then asks us to do them.

Because we know this, we can use this to assess if something is of God or not. When we hear others describe what God does and how He treats others, we can compare this to love to determine if it is valid and appropriate to ascribe it to God. For example, when others say that God predestines people to hell before they are even born and not given a chance to be redeemed, we can doubt it as being true because love would not do that to people. It is only fair that people be given an opportunity to prove themselves. When we hear others say that God only wants to save some and not everyone, we can doubt this as being true because that is not what love would do. God does not show partiality (Rom. 2:11; Col. 3:35; Acts 10:34; Eph. 6:9; Gal. 2:6). It would be unjust if God did not give people a chance. God cannot act in a manner that is untrue or inconsistent with His character. God is perfect in love. God's love is manifested by his absolute, pure, and loving motives. He cares about us, and it will always show.

Since God is love, we reflect God's character the most when we love others. This shows we know God, follow God, and try to glorify God in all we do. God receives no greater honor and praise than when we express love to others.

Agape Defined (Agapé•ἀγάπη• ag-ah'-pay)

So, let's now take a look at understanding what agape means. This is a divine type of love. This is the highest and purest form of love. The New Testament references agape 115 times. Biblical writers use God as the standard for true agape.

God is the very definition of the agape kind of love as agape is a core aspect of His character. God is the perfect example of what true and sacrificial love means. God's love in no sense is in conflict with his holiness, righteousness, justice, or even His wrath. Those who receive God's wrath are deserving of it. All of God's attributes are in perfect harmony. Everything God does is done with loving motives. God's love is so great and flawless that it is hard for us to comprehend.

The love of agape is a direct act of choice, an act of the will (intentional, a conscious choice) and does not need to be motivated by superficial appearance, emotional attraction, or a sentimental relationship. The love of agape is not based on pleasant emotions or good feelings that might result from a physical attraction or a familial bond. The love of agape extends beyond emotions. It's much more than an emotional reaction.

The love of agape is active. It demonstrates love through actions. Agape is the love of serving with humility and the purist kind of devotion. Agape requires faithfulness, commitment, and sacrifice. Agape seeks the well-being of others without basing it on what one can get in return. This kind of love, agape, reflects the very heartbeat of God.

Agape Is Unconditional Love

God's love as described in the Bible is clearly unconditional love. God's love is expressed toward everyone regardless of one's disposition or attitude toward Him at any given moment. In other words, God loves because it is His nature to love. Unlike human affection, God's love doesn't fluctuate. God does not care for us more when we have pleased Him or less at times when we have disappointed Him. God loves everyone all the time.

The unconditional nature of God's love is most clearly seen in the gospels. The gospel message is, in part, a story of divine rescue. As God considers the plight of His rebellious people, He determines to save them from their sin. This resolve is based on His love, not a particular aspect, quality, or action of a person. God does not place conditions on us for Him to love us.

It is important to note that God's love is a love that initiates. That is precisely what makes it unconditional. If God's love were conditional, then we would have to do something to earn or merit His love. We would have to somehow appease His wrath and cleanse ourselves of our sin before God would be able to love us. But that is not the biblical message. The truth is that God, motivated by love, moved unconditionally to save people from their sin. It is based on grace.

Agape Defined in 1 Corinthians 13

The apostle Paul provides a crystal clear treatise and explanation about the importance of love (agape) in 1 Corinthians 13. Here he spends some time defining love. He says love is the greatest quality we can ever strive to have in our lives. True love never ceases and never fails. Without love... well, let's just see what he says.

1 Corinthians 13:1–13:

> If I speak in the tongues of men or of angels, but do not have love, I am only a resounding gong or a clanging cymbal. If I have the gift of prophecy and can fathom all mysteries and all knowledge, and if I have a faith that can move mountains, but do not have love, I am nothing. If I give all I possess to the poor and give over my body to hardship that I may boast, but do not have love, I gain nothing.
>
> Love is patient, love is kind. It does not envy, it does not boast, it is not proud. It does not dishonor others, it is not self-seeking, it is not easily angered, it keeps no record of wrongs. Love does not delight in evil but rejoices with the truth. It always protects, always trusts, always hopes, always perseveres.
>
> Love never fails. But where there are prophecies, they will cease; where there are tongues, they will be stilled; where

there is knowledge, it will pass away. For we know in part and we prophesy in part, but when completeness comes, what is in part disappears. When I was a child, I talked like a child, I thought like a child, I reasoned like a child. When I became a man, I put the ways of childhood behind me. For now we see only a reflection as in a mirror; then we shall see face to face. Now I know in part; then I shall know fully, even as I am fully known.

And now these three remain: faith, hope and love. But the greatest of these is love.

What Do We Learn about Agape from 1 Corinthians 13?

Love is supreme. Love is about how we interact with each other. Love is the opposite of selfishness or self-centeredness. It is other-centered. Paul says that without love, our unique gifts and abilities are meaningless. Our acts of service are empty. Our big initiatives are futile. Our positive qualities are pointless. The significance of all of these important and great things hinges on love. He goes on to say that love is the greatest of all the virtues.

Even though we try hard to understand what it means that God is love, it is very likely that we only scratch the surface. This is a good thing, though. We all want a God who is so great that we can't fully comprehend the depth of His being. His love is so far beyond anything we can measure or imagine. This is something we all can celebrate!

2. God's Love for Us

Admittedly, it is difficult to distinguish between the notions of God being love and God loving us. One naturally and logically flows to the other.

The truth we learn from a balanced view of Scriptures is that God created us to love us. He loves us unconditionally. He cares deeply about the oppressed, the disadvantaged, the weak, and those who Jesus called the "least of these" in Matthew 25. We read in Matthew 12:20 where an Old Testament Scripture found in Isaiah 42:3 was quoted: "A bruised reed He will not break, and a smoldering wick He will not snuff out, till He has brought justice through to victory." Jesus cares about everyone, especially those who are struggling and what some call the outcasts of society.

We see the greatest manifestation of God's love for us by what He has done to make it possible for all of us to go to heaven to be with Him after this life. As the sole creator of everything, God gets to set the rules and boundaries for the kind of relationship we are to have with Him and what He expects from us. He set this up before the foundations of the world were made. God has done what is necessary for us to be reconciled with Him. He sent His son Jesus. There is no greater love than this. He gives us the option to choose life with Him or reject Him. **It's the biggest choice of our lives.** This is briefly explained in the follow passage of Scripture, the greatest expression of God's love, **John 3:16**:

> For God so loved the world that He gave His only begotten Son, that whoever believes in Him shall not perish, but have eternal life.

Listen to what many say about this Scripture:

1. John 3:16 is the North Star of the Bible. If you align your life with it, you can find the way home.[41]
2. John 3:16 is the Mount Everest of Scripture passages from God's Word.[42]
3. John 3:16 is the most important verse in the Bible.[43]
4. No other verse in the Bible so succinctly summarizes God's relationship with humanity and the way of salvation.[44]
5. The Protestant reformer Martin Luther called John 3:16 "the gospel in miniature."[45]
6. Biblical Commentator William Barclay wrote that John 3:16 is "the very essence of the Gospel."[46]
7. Gospel preacher, Robert Jackson, entitled John 3:16 in a sermon, "The greatest sentence ever written."[47]
8. Some consider John 3:16 as the "theme verse" for the entire Bible.[48]

Another powerful Scripture to highlight the love God has for us is highlighted in the following passage, **Romans 5:6–11**:

> You see, at just the right time, when we were still powerless, Christ died for the ungodly. Very rarely will anyone die for a righteous person, though for a good person someone might

possibly dare to die. But God demonstrates his own love for us in this: While we were still sinners, Christ died for us.

Since we have now been justified by his blood, how much more shall we be saved from God's wrath through him! For if, while we were God's enemies, we were reconciled to him through the death of his Son, how much more, having been reconciled, shall we be saved through his life! Not only is this so, but we also boast in God through our Lord Jesus Christ, through whom we have now received reconciliation.

Consider these additional Bible verses where God tells us how much He loves us.

1 John 3:1:

See what great love the Father has lavished on us, that we should be called children of God! And that is what we are! The reason the world does not know us is that it did not know him.

Being called children of God is something incredibly special. It relates to our relationship with God and our eternal destiny.

Ephesians 2:4–5:

But because of his great love for us, God, who is rich in mercy, made us alive with Christ even when we were dead in transgressions—it is by grace you have been saved.

Here the apostle Paul uses figurative language to express the depth of God's love. He uses the metaphor "dead in our transgressions." We are not literally dead. The word "dead" is used symbolically as a description of our spiritual status before we are forgiven and saved. God's love enabled us to become spiritually alive in Christ through the salvation process.

God's love is what should help sustain us in times of need. It means that God does care about each of us and gives us hope for a terrific life with Him after this one. Knowing God's love should be a source of great encouragement. It is the greatest reality in the whole wide world!

3. Our Love for God

Our love for God begins with His love for us. Understanding this makes all the difference in our motivation.

Achieving the motivation and frame of mind to love another can be challenging. The easy ones to love are those with whom we have a close and positive personal relationship, such as our family and good friends. We don't need to be taught or told to love them. Our love for them is like an automatic response. This is the kind of love that flows deep and wide. Most everyone easily experiences this.

Our love for God is based on the kind of relationship we have with Him. However, we must understand very clearly that God wants and demands everyone to establish a strong relationship with Him. That is why the Scriptures are so full of references to our love for God and, especially, the command that we love God with all our heart, soul, and mind. Obeying this command is only possible when we have a strong relationship with God.

The Greatest Commandment

Let's review the greatest command ever given by God to us humans. In **Matthew 22:34–40**, we read:

> Hearing that Jesus had silenced the Sadducees, the Pharisees got together. One of them, an expert in the law, tested him with this question: "Teacher, which is the greatest commandment in the Law?"

> Jesus replied: "'Love the Lord your God with all your heart and with all your soul and with all your mind.' This is the first and greatest commandment. And the second is like it: 'Love your neighbor as yourself.' All the Law and the Prophets hang on these two commandments."

Jesus tells us something incredibly profound. In response to a question, He gives us a clear and specific statement about the most important thing

God wants from us. If anything in all of Scripture should get our attention, it should be this! Out of 613 rules and regulations established by those in Old Testament times for helping the Israelites keep the commandments of God, Jesus summarizes their fulfillment in two commandments. A command is the highest level of obligation for obedience expected and demanded of Christians.

The Meaning of Heart, Soul, and Mind

The heart, soul, and mind represent the vastness of what we are as a person. Everything we are and have must be devoted to loving and serving God.

Let's look at the Greek words used for heart, soul, and mind.

Heart—

The Greek word used for heart is **kardia**, καρδία.[49] It is pronounced kar-dee'-ah. It means heart, mind, character, inner self, will, and intention. It refers to the affective center of our being, the desire-producer that makes us tick and motivates the decisions we make for determining how we live our lives. This word kardia is mentioned over 800 times in Scripture but never referring to the literal physical pump that drives the blood. That is, the word "heart" is only used figuratively.

Soul—

The Greek word used for soul is **psuché**, ψυχή.[50] It is pronounced psoo-khay'. It means (a) the vital breath, breath of life, (b) the human soul, (c) the soul as the seat of affections and will, (d) the self, and (e) a human person, an individual. It comes from the root word psyxō, which means "to breathe, blow" (which is the root of the English words "psyche," "psychology"). It relates to a person's distinct identity, one's unique personhood and individual personality. The soul is the direct aftermath of God breathing (blowing) His gift of life into a person, making them an ensouled being.

Mind—

The Greek word used for mind is **dianoia** (διάνοια).[51] It is pronounced dee-an'-oy-ah. It means our understanding, intellect, mind, and insight. It comes from the root words of (1) diá, "thoroughly, from side-to-side," which intensifies, (2) from noiéō, "to use the mind," and (3) from noús, "mind." It refers to movement from one side (of an issue) to the other to reach balanced conclusions; full-orbed reasoning, that is, dialectical thinking (the ability to see things from many perspectives) that literally reaches "across to the other side" of a matter. It relates to critical thinking, literally "thorough reasoning." Such reasoning is essential to loving the Lord and our neighbor.

So we can see that our heart, soul, and mind represent all of what we are in our reasoning and mental capacities for how we respond to the questions and issues of life. This is the max. This is the standard God set for us. Our efforts to love God this way will take a deep commitment.

How Much Love Is Enough?

We can ask, "How can we evaluate ourselves regarding the extent of our love for God?" Are we doing enough? What is enough? For example, are we to do "this" and "that," or are we to do it "this way" and "that way," or are we to do it "this amount" and "that amount" and then our efforts will be acceptable to God? We quickly can see that the words heart, soul, and mind are not exact descriptions. We are not given anchor points for how to measure all of this.

In the Old Testament times, the Israelite people had the Law. As mentioned earlier, to help ensure the Law was followed, there were 613 extra requirements added. They had the "this" and "thats." All of this fueled reasons to be judgmental, and we all know it was not possible to follow.

However, things are different for New Testament Christians. Commands and expectations include some measure of vagueness in how they are expressed to us now. This is typical for how we are asked or commanded to do things in the New Testament. There is a good reason why things are communicated this way.

When the Scriptures give us commands and directives, these are often general in focus and serve as principles for how we are to live our lives. The Scriptures are not about telling us specifically which person to marry, who the people are that we are to have deep personal relationships with in our lives, where to go to church and so on. The commands are often general in nature, all-encompassing guidelines for living. Again, these are given to us so we can be more like God. In response to being commanded to love others, there are no limits set on this. That's because God wants us to always be seeking to love others more. We never arrive at the limit.

4. Loving Our Neighbors as Ourselves

How easy is it for us to love others? Most people would answer, "It depends." So, what would be the variables? Well, again, it depends! Some might say it depends on how much we have in common with the person, how close we are to the person, if the person shares our values and beliefs, how engaging the person is with us, how often we get to be with the person, and so on.

Now let's consider this, would those responses be the kind of answers God wants to hear from us? Would that be an acceptable answer to Him? This hinges upon what we mean by "love." If we are talking about an emotionally based kind of love or a romantic kind of love, then yes, there are a lot of variables at play. However, God is not asking or commanding us to love others that way. God is asking for us to apply the agape kind of love to others. Now again, this makes all the difference.

Love Your Neighbor

The idea of loving our neighbor is elevated in importance when it is stated as the second greatest commandment by Jesus in **Matthew 22:37–40**. "Jesus replied: "'Love the Lord your God with all your heart and with all your soul and with all your mind." This is the first and greatest commandment. And the second is like it: "Love your neighbor as yourself." All the Law and the Prophets hang on these two commandments. '"

The apostle Paul mentions this in his letter to the Galatians.

Galatians 5:13–14:

> You, my brothers and sisters, were called to be free. But do not use your freedom to indulge the flesh; rather, serve one another humbly in love. For the entire law is fulfilled in keeping this one command: 'Love your neighbor as yourself.'

In the gospel of Luke, an expert in the law asked Jesus, "What must I do to inherit eternal life?" (Luke 10:25). Jesus then turned that question back on him and answered it by saying the following in **Luke 10:27**:

> He answered, "'Love the Lord your God with all your heart and with all your soul and with all your strength and with all your mind'; and, 'Love your neighbor as yourself.'"

Jesus then said the man answered correctly. Then the expert in the law asked Jesus,

"Who is my neighbor?" Jesus answered him by telling the story of the Good Samaritan in **Luke 10:30–37** as we read below.

> In reply Jesus said: "A man was going down from Jerusalem to Jericho, when he was attacked by robbers. They stripped him of his clothes, beat him and went away, leaving him half dead. A priest happened to be going down the same road, and when he saw the man, he passed by on the other side. So too, a Levite, when he came to the place and saw him, passed by on the other side. But a Samaritan, as he traveled, came where the man was; and when he saw him, he took pity on him. He went to him and bandaged his wounds, pouring on oil and wine. Then he put the man on his own donkey, brought him to an inn and took care of him. The next day he took out two denarii and gave them to the innkeeper. 'Look after him,' he said, 'and when I return, I will reimburse you for any extra expense you may have.'"

> "Which of these three do you think was a neighbor to the man who fell into the hands of robbers?"

> The expert in the law replied, "The one who had mercy on him."

> Jesus told him, "Go and do likewise."

This is a fairly short story made up by Jesus. Everyone present would understand the cultural context, which, for us, needs a good amount of explanation. I'll add some context to help us grasp the importance and huge scope of this story.

The expert in the law was out to test Jesus. He was not a sincere questioner. After answering correctly about what one must do to inherit eternal life, he then asks, "And who is my neighbor?" He was likely seeking to know what would be the least amount of neighbor-loving he would need to do. He, like many others, was used to measuring his righteousness by how well he conformed outwardly to the law. For first-century Judeans, it was crystal clear who a neighbor was. It would be another Judean. They were very ethnocentric. He was probably thinking which subset of his Judean brothers he would need to love.

When answering this question, Jesus took this opportunity to shake things up. Jesus launches into one of the most disruptive paradigm shifts a parable has ever attempted. He went boldly against the cultural standards of the time with this story to deliberately turn norms upside down. The story told to answer the expert in the law's question took a different twist than anyone expected. Jesus answers the question by explaining what neighbor love looks and acts like (i. e. , love your neighbor as yourself) in ways that will surprise and shock their minds.

As additional background to the story, there was tremendous hostility between the Jews and the Samaritans. In fact, Samaritans were hated by the Jewish people and vice versa.

The story begins by saying a man went down from Jerusalem to Jericho. The person traveling was beaten and left for dead on the side of the road. He is understood to be a Jewish man, a Judean. Everyone there knew about this dangerous path that was seventeen miles in length, having a desert terrain with caves and a lot of rocks. Having robbers show up was a typical occurrence. Everyone knew what the fate would be of the man left half dead. He was certain to die. When the sun would go down, either the cold would kill him or wild animals would.

Then Jesus introduces us to a priest and Levite who just walked on by the dying man. They were known to travel this road quite frequently. They also represented the religious leaders of the day. They knew better than to ignore this man. They made a big mistake. They knew their obligation was to show love and compassion to the needy. But they didn't.

Then Jesus astonishes everyone by introducing the real hero of the story, a Samaritan man. A Samaritan would have been the least likely person to help the man. No one back then would have even remotely imagined that this guy would be the hero because of the hatred between the Jews and the Samaritans. It's the part of the story that would be hard for anyone to believe. This Samaritan man did things that were unthinkable back then. He went out of his way to help the Jewish man. He bandaged his wounds, poured expensive oil and wine on him, put the man on his donkey, brought him to an inn, and took care of him for the night. The next day, he gave the inn-keeper money worth about two weeks' wages to provide for the man's needs. He even committed to return to continue helping the man.

The weight of Jesus's teaching was huge. He redefined who a neighbor is, thus putting great responsibility on everyone in the world. A neighbor would no longer just be about ethnicity, proximity, and a relationship with a person. This broader concept was earth-shaking. This would force every person to examine their heart, confront their prejudices, and be willing to get involved with others in need, even those who are disliked or detested.

This story is certainly upside-down from what people might have expected. The bad guys were supposed to be the good guys, and the good guy was supposed to be the bad guy.

When Jesus asked, "Which of the three was a neighbor to the man who fell into the hands of robbers?" the answer the attorney gave correctly was, "The one who had mercy on him." He couldn't even say the word "Samaritan." Jesus then said something very important that was earth-shaking back then and should capture our imaginations today. He said, "**Go and do likewise.**" Neighbor love has no boundaries just as God's love doesn't. This is a story that had to be told. It is for everyone in every generation and every nation. Jesus wants us to be doers. Our love for others must be evidenced by what we do for others. When others need our help, our love for them is tested.

Showing mercy is a mandate for all of us and an example of what loving others means. The question we can ask ourselves as Christians is this, "Are we hypocritical when we aren't merciful?"

We see from this story that there can be risks and costs involved in showing mercy, in loving others. Mercy does not often fall within the realm of our comfort zones. Being merciful can take us to intimidating places where we must rely on our faith and trust God that things will work out. Yes, serving our neighbors requires we take risks for the sake of love.

There is another way to look at this story. Some say that the Samaritan person is an archetype of Jesus. It can be like an allegory of what Jesus will be doing for us on the cross. It can symbolize the compassion and care Jesus has for mankind as we are ultimately left vulnerable, unable to help ourselves, and in desperate need. The Samaritan person is like Jesus in that he makes provision for the needy person and satisfies the requirements of righteousness and justice. He takes on the cost and inconvenience of caring for another as though the person is a close family member. The Good Samaritan looks beyond prejudice and cultural norms and saves this man's life. Jesus saves us from the consequences of sin and separation from God to eternal life.

Love Your Neighbor "As Yourself"

Let's dig a little deeper into what the second greatest commandment means. The phrase "love your neighbor as yourself" is specifically chosen by Jesus. It comes from the Old Testament passage from Leviticus19:18.

Here we see where loving ourselves is brought front and center into the Scriptures. What are we to make of this? Let's take a look at the following Scriptures which are related in some way to this idea.
We read in **Psalm 139:14**:

I praise you because I am fearfully and wonderfully made...

Wonderful is something to celebrate! We are all encouraged, knowing we are made in such a special and unique way (Gen. 1:27–31).
We read in **Ephesians 5:29**:

After all, no one ever hated their own body, but they feed
and care for their body, just as Christ does the church...

Here we see that caring for our body is equated with Jesus caring for the church. Loving our bodies is like the love Jesus has for the church. This has to relate to a positive, constructive, and sacrificial love, not a self-centered, conceited kind of love.
We read in **Ephesians 2:10**:

For we are God's handiwork, created in Christ Jesus to do
good works, which God prepared in advance for us to do.

The idea of being God's handiwork implies we were crafted into the beings we are with vision, design and precision for a meaningful purpose. God would only refer to tremendous products of His making as His handiwork! No other created beings share this status. We are uniquely God's masterpiece.

From these passages we get the clear message that yes, we are very special, we must love ourselves, and with this, we must be humble in our attitudes that should impact the way we treat others.

The Golden Rule

One of the prominent ways to look at loving others as we love ourselves is expressed in what we know as the "Golden Rule." This is found in **Matthew 7:12:**

> So in everything, do to others what you would have them
> do to you, for this sums up the Law and the Prophets.

Here we are called to treat others as we want to be treated. This is based on the reality that we all have a deep love for ourselves. This would be the only basis for making this comment. This is one way we use self-love to motivate us to love others and treat others well. How important is the Golden Rule? It sums up what we need to know about the Law and the Prophets. That is huge!

The Importance of Self-Love

When Jesus says we are to love our neighbors as ourselves, He is saying that self-love is a pre-requisite for loving others. Self-love is the basis for loving others. We can't love others if we don't love ourselves. Loving ourselves is the foundation for a purposeful and meaningful life. We can't love others and we can't take care of others unless we love and take care of ourselves. God knows all of this because He made us. We have to know our value to appreciate what God has made. God wants us and others to appreciate His handiwork in making us, to be clear on how magnificent and wonderful we are.

Self-love is related to self-worth and self-esteem. These qualities drive our efforts. They are some of our greatest motivations. If we don't love ourselves or esteem ourselves highly, what is the impact of this on our lives? Two words: not good. People with low self-esteem are not high achievers. They settle for less because they don't see themselves deserving more. With low self-esteem, there is little courage and resilience.

Having self-love ties into our basic instincts, including how we automatically try to protect ourselves from harm and seek our best interests. Self-love is a part of our nature as humans. I believe this also relates to the notion that there is a lot of goodness in each of us. There is a lot to love about ourselves. We can, indeed, celebrate how wonderfully we are made!

Part of the idea of loving ourselves involves taking care of ourselves in the major areas of life. We must take care of ourselves physically by eating right, exercising regularly, sleeping/resting as we should, keeping ourselves free from harm and illness, and so on. We must take care of ourselves medically, which is related to physically. We must take care of ourselves emotionally and mentally. There are many psychological and psychiatric issues to which many are vulnerable and can greatly impact our functioning. When we are psychologically healthy, we can have the best life possible, that is, one with healthy relationships, good jobs, happy social life, and so on. We need to take care of ourselves socially, which is related to emotional health. We must take care of ourselves spiritually. That is what this whole book is about! We get much energy from having our lives in good shape and in "proper working order."

Our self-love is the strongest and broadest motivation we have. God knows the power of mankind's inner motivation and how strong this can be. We can accomplish a tremendous amount using our intrinsic will power. This is something that is often downplayed regarding spiritual matters in order to accent the power of God in our lives. In the partnership relationship we have with God, both forces are valuable, God and us.

There's a saying that the best thing a father can do for his children is to love his wife. Similarly, the best thing we all can do for others is to love ourselves.

5. Loving Others as Christ Has Loved Us

There is another very important variable when it comes to loving others. Jesus referred to this as a new idea in the gospel of John.

John 13:34:

> A new command I give you: Love one another. As I have loved you, so you must love one another.

There are two words in Greek for the word "new." One is "**Neos**," and refers to that which is new in time, that which is youngest or recent. Another is "**Kainos**," and describes that which is new in quality and not found exactly like this before.[52] "Kainos" is what the apostle John uses here.

The old commandment was to "love your neighbor as yourself" (Lev. 19:18). Jesus now gives His disciples a new standard: we are to love each other **as He has loved us**. This perspective of love takes our relationships with one another to a higher level. This relates to a deeper quality of love. It appears that Jesus's disciples have much to figure out about this new kind of love. They are about to find out just how deep this love is when Jesus goes to the cross.

Jesus Loved with Humility

This kind of love also relates to humility. Jesus showed incredible humility when He allowed Himself to be treated so badly for our sake through the ordeal He endured. Humility is an attitude that comes from a position of strength, not weakness. Jesus was the greatest and strongest person ever to live. We can learn that humility is required for us to love others deeply.

Jesus Loved Unconditionally

To love others as Jesus loved us requires us to grow in the ability to love others unconditionally. It's not about people meeting all of our demands and expectations before we love them. They don't have to think like us or have the qualities we want before we love them. It is clear that we are to love unconditionally. There is no one mentioned in the Scriptures we are not expected to love. Not our enemies, people of little social importance, those with terrible illnesses or deformities, those mentally challenged, strangers, those with no power or influence... no one. When we are demanded to love, we are not to ask questions like: "What's in it for me? What do I get out of it?" The truth is, it's not about us. We love because it's the right thing to do in all circumstances.

Having said all of this, how are we doing in the challenge to love unconditionally? Is it really possible for us to love everyone unconditionally? I'm sure many would say no. We must admit that this is a very high bar to reach. Even so, we should always strive toward this goal and ask God to help us. We'll likely do well with some people and fall short with others.

Loving unconditionally is about opening our heart to all people under all conditions and in all circumstances. Maybe we can only do this with the help of the Holy Spirit. The goal needs to be that we never stop trying. Again remember, we are talking about the agape kind of love.

Jesus Loved with Greater Love

There is a saying about love that goes like this: "The true measure of love is what one is willing to give up for it." This relates to sacrifice. Jesus sacrificed it all for us.

Jesus said in **John 15:13**:

> Greater love has no one than this, that he lay down his life
> for his friends.

This certainly is the greatest kind of love. It is how Jesus loves us. He made the ultimate sacrifice. This now becomes an example of the extent to which we should strive to love others.

Jesus takes the charge to love others to a very challenging level in **Matthew 5:43–46**:

> You have heard that it was said, "Love your neighbor and hate your enemy." But I tell you, love your enemies and pray for those who persecute you, that you may be children of your Father in heaven. He causes his sun to rise on the evil and the good, and sends rain on the righteous and the unrighteous. If you love those who love you, what reward will you get? Are not even the tax collectors doing that?

Jesus doesn't want us to only do what is easy. Anyone can do that. Jesus is looking for a deeper commitment. When Jesus brings up the need to love our enemies, He goes directly to the hardest ones for us to love. This is major. For some, this may appear very difficult if not impossible. This is certainly a big challenge for all of us.

We can only imagine what the world would be like if all Christians could be successful in loving our enemies. What would we see? It certainly would be interesting if there was a study on the effects of this. We do see some of this when people forgive those who have deeply hurt them. Enemies are often those who mistreat and hurt us deeply.

Loving Others God's Way

What will we see us doing if we, indeed, love other people God's way?

- Concern for their spiritual and physical well-being.
- Seek to influence others for God.
- Display the fruit of the Spirit to them.
- Be willing to sacrifice to help them. Give them our time and attention as we serve them (One way to spell love is t-i-m-e.).
- Be willing to give of our money to help others as we can.
- Getting involved in people's lives as we can.
- Remember, people don't care how much we know until they know how much we care.
- Treat others with respect no matter their status in life.
- Be an encourager.
- Take the initiative to get conflicts resolved.
- Get rid of our unloving ways, such as being judgmental, discriminatory, arrogant, selfish, indifferent, insincere, dishonest, hurtful, and generally uncaring.

Conclusion

I would say that most of us think of loving others in the context of a relationship we have with them, such as our family, friends, and others close to us. However, the emphasis to love is often focused toward strangers, to people with whom we don't have an ongoing relationship and even to those we don't like, such as our enemies. There is no one we are not to love.

We need to have a heart that cares about all people; a heart that becomes compassionate when we see suffering and need; a heart that is touched by God so that in following God, we show the love He wants us to show, the agape kind of love; and a heart that is softened by the grace we've been given and empowered by the Holy Spirit's working within us.

A word of caution may be helpful here. We do need to be careful as well. Our hearts can be hardened by the tough experiences we have in life. We must not let these cause us to wander away from God. Difficulties in life are not a sign that God does not care.

The agape kind of love is really about action. It is what we do to and for others. With love being commanded, we know that love must be seen. There should be obvious evidence of our love that is easy for everyone to see. We need to show love to others by what we do and not just by the words we utter. Words are not enough. There must be clear and convincing proof of our loving actions.

Love is one of the attributes of God within us and is evidence of our faith. Others must be able to know we are Christians by the way we love one another (John 13:35). The early church was often noted for the way they loved others. Their love was a witness to the authenticity of the gospel message that drew people to explore the benefits of following Christ. In many ways, the love we have for God and Jesus is demonstrated in the love we have for others.

We can grow in our love for God and others as we meditate upon the Scriptures and the truth of the messages presented in this chapter. Love will grow as we connect more deeply with our motivation to put our love into action.

CHAPTER 4

Joy

Living beyond Our Circumstances

"I have told you this so that my joy may be in you and that
your joy maybe complete."

—John 15:11

"But rejoice inasmuch as you participate in the sufferings
of Christ, so that you may be overjoyed when his glory
is revealed."

—1 Peter 4:1

We now come to joy, the second "fruit of the Spirit "mentioned in Galatians 5:22–23. Many may think this is the easiest one of the nine qualities to exhibit. After all, isn't joy an automatic response to the positive circumstances in our lives? We easily have joy. No big deal.

The kind of joy just referenced is the emotional response of joy. This comes from the many pleasant experiences we have in various aspects of life. However, this is not the sum total of what is meant by biblical joy. There is much more to it.

We will see in this chapter that, in many cases, joy is more than just an emotional response. It is also based upon a deeply rooted belief system that guides our lives and changes the way we respond to situations. This deeply rooted belief system can cause us to understand and interpret circumstances differently than just reacting emotionally. We'll unpack this as we progress through this chapter.

The Basis of Our Joy

The ultimate basis of our joy is in the coming of Jesus into the world, the purpose of His incarnation. Jesus is Immanuel, God with us. With the birth of Jesus, an angel told the shepherds living out in the fields nearby the following:

Luke 2:10–12:

> But the angel said to them, "Do not be afraid. I bring you good news that will cause great joy for all the people. Today in the town of David a Savior has been born to you; he is the Messiah, the Lord. This will be a sign to you: You will find a baby wrapped in cloths and lying in a manger."

This is, indeed, the greatest news of all time! It is the basis of great joy for all people. God, in His love for all mankind, sent His son to earth with a tremendous mission: to save people from their sins (Matt. 1:21). This would culminate with Jesus dying on the cross and being resurrected from the dead for our salvation.

The apostle Paul describes it this way in **Romans 5:6–11:**

> You see, at just the right time, when we were still powerless, Christ died for the ungodly. Very rarely will anyone die for a righteous person, though for a good person someone might possibly dare to die. But God demonstrates his own love for us in this: While we were still sinners, Christ died for us.

> Since we have now been justified by his blood, how much more shall we be saved from God's wrath through him! For if, while we were God's enemies, we were reconciled to him through the death of his Son, how much more, having been reconciled, shall we be saved through his life! Not only is this so, but we also boast in God through our Lord Jesus Christ, through whom we have now received reconciliation.

Because of all this, every Christian should seek to live a life worthy of the Lord and please Him in every way. We should seek to bear good fruit through our daily interactions and continually grow deeper in our knowledge and love of God. This is the foundation of our spiritual joy. We experience joy not because of happy circumstances but because of the hope we have in God's love and promises, especially because of our future eternal destiny with God. This joy comes from some place deeper than an attitude based on circumstances.

Let's review what the apostle Paul says about this.

Colossians 1:9–12:

> For this reason, since the day we heard about you, we have not stopped praying for you. We continually ask God to fill you with the knowledge of his will through all the wisdom and understanding that the Spirit gives, so that you may live a life worthy of the Lord and please him in every way: bearing fruit in every good work, growing in the knowledge of God, being strengthened with all power according to his glorious might so that you may have great endurance and patience, and giving joyful thanks to the Father, who has qualified you to share in the inheritance of his holy people in the kingdom of light.

The purpose of being full of knowledge, wisdom, and understanding is to help us live our lives worthy of the Lord. Paul's prayer involves asking us to bear fruit in every good work. Paul's prayer asks for us to have endurance and patience through being strengthened with all power according to His glorious might. Paul's prayer asks us to give joyful thanks to the Father who qualifies us to share in the inheritance of His holy people.

What a prayer! For this prayer to be actualized in the lives of believers would be a source of great joy! It is a joy based on what Jesus has done for us, not upon what we happen to experience at any given moment. It is a joy that is beyond our circumstances.

For joy to be listed in Galatians 5:22–23 among eight other qualities that are far from simple and easy to achieve should give us all pause. We must seek to look deeper into what joy is all about. We should expect that increasing our joy will require a dedicated effort just as with the other qualities.

A Few Scriptures on Joy

The New Testament Scriptures are full of encouragement for Christians to develop many skills, godly character, and habits as well as proper attitudes, including being joyful. The following are a couple of these passages.

1 Thessalonians 5:16–18:

> Rejoice always, pray continually, give thanks in all circumstances; for this is God's will for you in Christ Jesus.

Philippians 4:4–7:

> Rejoice in the Lord always. I will say it again: Rejoice! Let your gentleness be evident to all. The Lord is near. Do not be anxious about anything, but in every situation, by prayer and petition, with thanksgiving, present your requests to God. And the peace of God, which transcends all understanding, will guard your hearts and your minds in Christ Jesus.

Romans 12:12:

> Be joyful in hope, patient in affliction, faithful in prayer.

After Jesus tells His disciples that He is going away, He acknowledges they will grieve. He then says, "but your grief will turn to joy" (John 16:20). Jesus then tells an analogy of a woman giving birth and how, when her baby is born, she forgets the anguish of the birthing process because of the joy her child brings to her. He then says in verse 22 that no one can take away our joy. Yes, no one and no circumstance can take away our joy. Because of our hope, it is always present.

Understanding Joy

Being joyful is one of the qualities that should characterize all Christians. We have deep and abiding reasons to be joyful. It is something we all should embrace each day.

As we discussed earlier, we all experience emotional joy regularly in our everyday lives. It is very common to our human experience. That is why many people could assume that joy is a simple concept to understand.

However, when it comes to understanding how joy is often used in the Scriptures, we will see a different kind of joy emerge. The emotional joy we often experience is one that is focused on our circumstances. It is what all people can identify with regardless of their level of spirituality.

We find this kind of joy defined in the *Webster's Dictionary* described as the following:

> A glad feeling; happiness; great pleasure; delight. Joy is anything causing such feelings.[53]

From this, we can see that joy is the emotion evoked by well-being, success, good fortune, and the prospect of possessing what one desires. Again, what we see here is an emotional experience associated with the good things happening to us. We know from the world's point of view that joy and happiness are used interchangeably. All of this is good and valid. However, we must ask, does this accurately describe the breadth and extent of joy the Bible is talking about? We must accept that we need to understand terms more than from just a worldly point of view.

As we try to convey meaning to each other, words matter a great deal. Getting words wrong and misunderstanding the meaning of words is serious business and can have significant consequences. In our casual conversations, many of us don't always choose the best words or choose our words precisely. However, for the biblical writers, this is not the case. Words are chosen carefully each and every time. (How could it be otherwise? If we can't trust that the words are always accurate, how could we then trust the Bible? There are many resources that can be found for further study on this.)

As we seek to understand the Scriptures, we must realize they are based on an expanded view to life, not just from the natural world's perspective. The Bible is all about introducing us to God, learning spiritual truths and important concepts to help us all develop an authentic relationship with Him. Therefore, only those who develop a strong, deep, and lasting faith can really see the full meaning of biblical teachings in the way in which they are intended.

A Biblical Perspective of Joy

So, let's look at the idea of joy from a biblical perspective. This will take into consideration the Greek words used for joy and how joy fits in with the eternal perspective we should maintain as we interact with life.

The best way to understand the kind of joy we are encouraged to have in the New Testament Scriptures is to research the words used in the passages for "joy." The Greek word "**chara**" (pronounced khar-ah') is the primary word used for joy in the New Testament. I found that it is used about fifty times in the New Testament. The Greek word for "rejoice" is "**chairó**" (pronounced khah'-ee-ro) and it is a derivative of the word chara. Chairó is used thirty-seven times in the New Testament.

The definition given for chara is the following:

> **Chara** is a Greek noun which describes joy as a feeling of inner gladness, delight or rejoicing. Joy in the New Testament is virtually always used to signify a feeling of "happiness" that is based on spiritual realities. Joy is an inner gladness; a deep seated pleasure. It is a depth of assurance and confidence that ignites a cheerful heart. It is a cheerful heart that leads to cheerful behavior. It is based on an awareness of God's grace and favor.[54,55]

I've reviewed all of the fifty passages of Scripture that use this word for joy. It is clear that there are two ways this word is applied. In several verses, it refers to an emotion. In the majority of situations, it involves a deeper spiritual meaning than joy as an emotional reaction coming from pleasant situations.

For understanding the word from a deeper spiritual meaning, this joy is tied to a broader perspective, an eternal perspective. This joy represents responding to external circumstances with inner contentment because we know we overcome the world (John 6:33). It is joy which is anchored in the facts of our faith and based on a confident mindset. This kind of joy is based on reasons, evidence, and conclusions, not simple emotions. It is joy that is tied to our deep and lasting faith, our faithful nature. It is part of the transformation we experience when we are born again. It's a reflection of something deep inside us. It is part of our godly nature. It comes from the hope we have for a home in heaven. It comes from a process taking place in our minds as important ideas are remembered and claimed.

Theopedia, an online encyclopedia of biblical Christianity, defines joy more as "a state of mind and an orientation of the heart. It's a settled state of contentment, confidence and hope."[56]

For this kind of joy, it takes a spiritual and eternal perspective to be able to understand and appreciate its full meaning. This perspective allows us to receive strength and persevere in all kinds of circumstances. Consider the following passages:

1 Peter 1:8–9:

> Though you have not seen him, you love him; and even though you do not see him now, you believe in him and are filled with an inexpressible and glorious joy, for you are receiving the end result of your faith, the salvation of your souls.

Hebrews 12:1–3:

> Therefore, since we are surrounded by such a great cloud of witnesses, let us throw off everything that hinders and the sin that so easily entangles. And let us run with perseverance the race marked out for us, fixing our eyes on Jesus, the pioneer and perfecter of faith. For the joy set before him he endured the cross, scorning its shame, and sat down at the right hand of the throne of God. Consider him who endured such opposition from sinners, so that you will not grow weary and lose heart.

1 Peter 4:12–13:

> Dear friends, do not be surprised at the fiery ordeal that has come on you to test you, as though something strange were happening to you. But rejoice inasmuch as you participate in the sufferings of Christ, so that you may be overjoyed when his glory is revealed

I like to think of biblical joy as an abiding, calming assurance that no matter what happens, we are eternally safe and secure thanks to the confidence and endurance of our faith and trust in what Jesus has done for us. This is the kind of joy biblical authors talk about having in difficult times. Consider the following Scriptures that refer to this:

James 1:2–4:

> Consider it pure joy, my brothers and sisters, whenever you face trials of many kinds, because you know that the testing of your faith produces perseverance. Let perseverance finish its work so that you may be mature and complete, not lacking anything.

1 Peter 1:3–7:

> Praise be to the God and Father of our Lord Jesus Christ! In his great mercy he has given us new birth into a living hope through the resurrection of Jesus Christ from the dead, and into an inheritance that can never perish, spoil or fade. This inheritance is kept in heaven for you, who through faith are shielded by God's power until the coming of the salvation that is ready to be revealed in the last time. In all this you greatly rejoice, though now for a little while you may have had to suffer grief in all kinds of trials. These have come so that the proven genuineness of your faith—of greater worth than gold, which perishes even though refined by fire—may result in praise, glory and honor when Jesus Christ is revealed.

The only way to make sense of these passages is by interpreting the word joy not as happiness but as being tied to our understanding of what Jesus has done, how we overcome the world, and how we have changed and have a hope for life eternal with Jesus. This is something worth more than gold! God is not asking us to take emotional pleasure in our pain and suffering. Joy in these passages does not come from our circumstances. Frustrations and difficulties don't have to rob us of joy. Also, God gives us strength and power as we deal with all of our struggles. All of this brings true joy to our lives!

The Meaning of Rejoice

Consider the following Scriptures using the Greek word "chairó" for rejoice.

Matthew 4:12:

Rejoice and be glad, because great is your reward in heaven...

John 16:22:

So with you: Now is your time of grief, but I will see you again and you will rejoice [chairo], and no one will take away your joy [chara].

Acts 5:41:

The apostles left the Sanhedrin, rejoicing because they had been counted worthy of suffering disgrace for the Name.

1 Peter 4:13:

But rejoice inasmuch as you participate in the sufferings of Christ, so that you may be overjoyed when his glory is revealed.

These and other passages with the word "rejoice" in them communicate a similar message of how our rejoicing emerges from a deeper place than just emotions.

Joy as Happiness

The other kind of joy the Greek word "chara" refers to sometimes is the pleasant feelings derived from a situation or circumstance. However, there is some clarification needed to fully understand this.

There is a debate in the Christian community regarding whether it is appropriate to define joy as happiness. There are ways to make the case that joy is more than merely feeling happy. The major reason why was just discussed above. However, some passages do refer to joy as a feeling of happiness.

The word happiness comes from the Latin word "hap," which relates to chance. It is a spontaneous response to temporary pleasures. Most people define happiness as getting what one wants in the moment. It's about being pleased by what is going on. It's a reaction to one's circumstances. Happiness is based on feelings derived from the situation and circumstances at any given time. It is often an emotional experience attributed to short-term pleasures and thus, creating short-term joy.

We know there are people who like to elevate the role of happiness as being very important in their lives. They try to use this to justify their behaviors and decisions by saying that God wants them to be happy. It's as if they believe God says the pursuit of happiness is okay to be one of life's major priorities. As an example, God wants me to be happy so I will have an extra-marital affair with another woman I find enjoyable to be around. Much of this kind of happiness has its roots in selfishness.

If happiness is our goal, then our standards and guidelines for living would fluctuate from situation-to-situation. We would be chasing happiness, which could mean anything that makes us happy is God's will, which is not the case! If happiness is our guiding principle, then we could avoid all things that don't make us happy, all things unpleasant. There would be no sacrifice, no suffering for doing good, and so on. Can we be happy when we are having struggles, trials, intense stress, suffering, and so on? Emotional happiness does not occur with these unhappy circumstances.

However, if circumstances have an influence or control over all our joy, then joy could not be experienced many times. Sad circumstances don't produce emotional joy. Whereas happiness is tied to current circumstances, a deeper sense of joy is tied to eternal circumstances. Joy and sorrow (the absence of joy) can exist together concurrently because of this broader perspective.

Joy as a Deeper Perspective Not Based on Circumstances

Again, joy can be viewed as a deeply held belief. This kind of joy is focused on what we receive by being followers of Christ. This joy relates to salvation associated with our faith so that we can have joy no matter what our circumstances, even in challenging and difficult circumstances. Joy can be the inward peace that is not affected by our situations. This joy comes from a right relationship with God, from a clear understanding and deep conviction of our hope for heaven.

Circumstances of life vary often between being positive and negative, happy and stressful, and encouraging and discouraging. However, the assurance of being with Christ one day never changes with circumstances. It is in this fact that our joy is anchored. This is how the apostle Paul could be so joyful and sing songs while he was being tortured in prison (Acts 16:16–40). We don't choose to become Christians because we want an easy life filled with circumstances that always make us happy. There will be times of sacrifice, suffering, and difficulty because we are Christians.

As mentioned above, pursuing happiness should not be one of our goals in life. In another sense, joy should not be pursued directly either. Joy is a byproduct of godly living. Joy comes as a result of being and remaining in a right relationship with God. It becomes part of our new godly nature.

Considering all of this, we can say that God is the source of our joy. This started with bringing Jesus to earth and the promise of joy we can have because of this. Jesus has made our joy complete (John 15:11). He has done all that needs to be done for us to have joy.

Joy and Love

Joy is possible because we know of God's love for us and the hope we have in Jesus. This means that joy is for the taking for those who accept Jesus as their Lord and Savior. Our joy is expressed by our love for God and others. We find joy by being engaged with life. Joy comes in what we celebrate with others. Joy comes from being around those we love. We find joy in serving those in need because of our love for them. We find joy in giving money and our time and effort because of the love in our hearts. Joy comes when a person we've been leading to the Lord accepts Jesus as their Lord and Savior and becomes born again. We find joy when problems are solved. Joy comes from living a love-based life.

The Holy Spirit dwelling within us is perfectly capable of guiding us away from the temptations of the enemy (Satan) and toward the grace and mercy and joy that can only be found in Jesus. This is how we can rejoice in the Lord always. Embrace the unconditional love of God and be filled with joy.

God and Our Emotions

Have you ever questioned whether God would command us to have a specific emotion or, on the other hand, to not have a specific emotion? If so, which ones and how can this be?

Emotions are initial reactions to circumstances. They don't have a moral component to them. They are neither right nor wrong from a moral perspective. This is largely because they are not felt intentionally or on purpose; they just come innocently and quickly at first. Now, to remain in an unhealthy emotional state without taking action for improvement can be another issue.

Emotions are feelings generated by each person based upon a number of personal reasons. Emotions are based on our cognitive processing of something that has happened. Feelings are preceded by our thinking about what just occurred. Sometimes, feelings come very quickly in response to a circumstance. In these situations, our brains quickly trigger an emotional response. These emotions can come upon us so quickly that it appears they are immediate or automatic responses. However, these responses come from past learning due to one having experienced something similar before or human instinct. Some emotional responses come from being primed to have them. For instance, being afraid of the dark can come from the taunting of others by encouraging one to be afraid due to fictional bad things that will happen, that is, the boogie man will get you.

An emotion can be a complex psychological event that involves a mixture of reactions. An emotion is often intertwined with mood, temperament, personality, and disposition. Again, cognition, the workings of our mind, plays an important part in our emotional reactions. We can generate an emotion just by thinking about something emotional that happened in our past. On the other hand, one would be hard-pressed to feel an emotion by thinking about something one has never experienced before.

What provokes a feeling in one person may not in another. We each have our own emotional makeup. It can be based on past experiences that have made us more sensitive, and possibly conditioned, on how to react to a situation. Emotional reactions can be based on our socialization while growing up. This comes from how our parents and others treated us and how we learned to respond to our environment.

For example, some people have been raised in a dysfunctional family where they experienced much pain and disappointment to the point that they were forced to learn how to emotionally protect themselves from the emotional pain. The unspoken rules in some dysfunctional families are "don't trust, don't feel, and don't talk." People learn to cope by dulling their emotional reactions in these situations. If you were raised in a moderate to severely dysfunctional family, you learned over time how to adjust and cope. However, the skills and habits you learned in order to cope with those situations are uniquely suited to be effective in dysfunctional situations. Those same habits do not work well in healthy situations.

Emotions can affect our physiology. Emotions can range from mild to intense. Brain and neurological activity are associated with our emotions. That is why psychotropic medication can be used to help with emotional issues.

So we can see that emotions are a complex concept. Given all of this, I don't see how God would command us to have an emotion or forbid us from having an emotion.

As parents, we can have fun with our young children, asking them to show differing facial expressions of emotions. We can ask them to show a happy face, a sad face, a surprised face, and so on. However, we wouldn't expect them to authentically feel those emotions at our request.

Dealing with Troubling Emotions

In my counseling with people regarding emotional issues, I use the cognitive-behavioral therapy (CBT) approach. This involves changing our thinking and the assumptions we have about our circumstances. The focus is, therefore, on what is going on in our minds, not our emotions. This is how we can get a handle on our emotions. There has been a good deal of research on this therapeutic approach showing its effectiveness for dealing with emotions, such as worry, anxiety, panic attacks, and depression, among other emotional issues. [57], [58]

The CBT approach tries to change the unhealthy habits of the mind. Many of our thoughts are distorted and self-defeating. So often, we find we jump to conclusions too quickly, which can then affect our reactions and behaviors. What we need to do instead is to stop and spend time thinking before reacting when circumstances arise that trigger emotions.

The images below with the A-B-C triangles (Figure 1 and Figure 2) are a simple way to illustrate the CBT approach. Figure 1 illustrates that once there is an activating event, which "A" represents (something happens), people then usually go directly to "C," where they respond almost automatically and by habit. This includes an emotional reaction or a behavioral reaction, or both.

What we really need to do is to stop going from "A" directly to "C" and, instead, go from "A" to "B" (Figure 2). At "B" is where we spend time analyzing the situation and what we are thinking. We look at assumptions we are making, we look at our "self-talk," and we examine all of this in our minds. We need to discover the distorted and unhealthy thinking and replace it with healthy thinking (the truth). What we want to accomplish is to be aware of what is truly going on so we can decide how we can best respond. Then we go to "C" and respond appropriately.

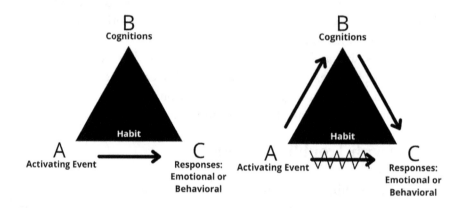

Many of the emotional issues we have are a result of faulty assumptions and beliefs we maintain. These can come from past experiences and how we've learned to cope. Correcting these faulty assumptions can help us respond more appropriately.

Conclusion—Living Joyful Lives God's Way

Again, I believe the kind of joy the Scriptures ask us to have is often not of the emotional kind. It is the deep-seated, firmly established joy which is anchored in the facts of our faith and the strength of our convictions. It is joy based upon our understanding of what God has done for us and how God can use our circumstances to make us better people. The Scriptures tell us of the benefits of enduring the trials of life for a reason. We use this information in how we respond to life.

We are asked to do many things in the Scriptures as part of the process of our becoming spiritually mature, healthy, and strong. Being asked and reminded to be joyful encourages us to have healthy spiritual attitudes in the course of our daily living. It also reminds us of the deep-seated joy we have that becomes part of our godly character.

When the Scriptures ask us to be joyful, they are not intended to be threats of punishment if we are not as joyful as we could or should be. These requests are to encourage us with positive motivation. This principle applies to many kinds of encouragements and appeals in Scripture, such as not to worry or not to be fearful.

As human beings, we all strive to pursue and create joy and happiness in our lives. It appears to be a universal drive in all people. It's related to self-love and self-preservation. Given our knowledge of the contemporary world, we know that achieving joy and happiness is easier in some nations, like the USA. Contrast America with Communist countries. The more freedoms we have and the more laws that protect these freedoms, the more that joy and happiness can thrive.

Addressing the topic of joy and happiness should have the effect of a wake-up call for some who are looking for joy in the wrong places. We know this is very true with those who are unbelievers and don't focus on things of the Spirit. The truth is, we all can get caught up in our materialistic world. A discussion of joy might be a good time to review our lives and where our priorities lie.

Let's consider the subcultures that exist in America and the world. Religion is a subculture. Christianity is one branch of the religious subculture. What is different for Christians? We seek joy and happiness based on a specific worldview, through the eyes of God, our Creator. God knows all about joy and happiness. Joy is a feature of God's wonderful attributes. God created us to be like Him. He wants us to enjoy life from a godly worldview. This makes us different in many ways from others who do not share this perspective. It certainly appears true that God made all humans with an insatiable appetite for joy and happiness but one that needs to be governed by godly guidance and boundaries.

As discussed in this chapter, we find joy from a right relationship with God. Joy is a byproduct of godly living. We learn we can receive strength from our faith and convictions. We learn about joy from how the Scriptures tell us how to live godly, joyful lives. We learn from the examples of Jesus, the apostles, and other great people of faith. We are blessed to have the Holy

Spirit as a helper from God. Again, all of this makes us different from our human companions who do not share our worldview. Our joy is not mostly about ourselves, our selfish ways, and our self-interests but about God and how we delight in God.

There was a popular song written by Bob Merrill for the 1961 Broadway musical *Carnival.* It was named: "Love Makes the World Go Round." Love gives meaning to so much. What would life be like if there was no love? No one could imagine this. Without love, there would be no joy.

Life without joy would be nothing less than depressing and hopeless. Here is where we find a strong connection of love to our joy.

Let's finish by considering some of the benefits of joyful living from a Christian worldview.

- Joy is important to God. Joy brings us closer to God each day.
- Joy is evidence of the power of the Holy Spirit in us.
- Joy gives us strength, energizes us, and gives us the ability to persevere through the difficult experiences of life.
- Joy is contagious, spreads to others, and is a sign of spiritual maturity.
- Joy enables us to experience life positively because of the eternal perspective our faith brings to our circumstances.
- Joy in our circumstances brings intermittent happiness to our lives and brightens each day.
- Joy helps us celebrate God, our faith, and the hope we have for a future with God after this life.
- Joy validates that our faith is true and keeps us focused and connected to the reasons for our faith, which keeps us encouraged.
- Joy helps us maintain the right kind of godly attitudes and affirms there is plenty to enjoy in Christianity.
- Joy helps us stand on the promises of God.

True joy and happiness begin and end with God.

CHAPTER 5

Peace

Blessed Are the Peacemakers

For he himself is our peace, who has made the two groups
one and has destroyed the barrier, the dividing wall of
hostility, by setting aside in his flesh the law with its
commands and regulations. His purpose was to create in
himself one new humanity out of the two, thus making
peace, and in one body to reconcile both of them to God
through the cross, by which he put to death their hostility.

—Ephesians 2:14–16

"If it is possible, as far as it depends on you, live at peace
with everyone."

—Romans 12:18

"Blessed are the peacemakers, for they shall be
called sons of God."

—Matthew 5:9

We now come to peace, the third "fruit of the Spirit" mentioned by the apostle
Paul in Galatians 5:22–23. We know peace is a concept that is broad and
multifaceted. Having peace in life can be very challenging as much of this is

impacted by circumstances beyond a person's control. That is why the apostle Paul says above, "as far as it depends on you, live at peace with everyone."

Peace is one of the greatest desires of loving people. Love is what makes peace possible. Without love, much of the motivation for peace vanishes. This again underscores how love is the most important virtue in life.

Look at the last two Scriptures above. One says, "as far as it depends on you," and the other says "Blessed are the peacemakers." Does this sound like it is talking to us, Christian people, to do what is being asked? This is yet another bit of evidence that it is not the Holy Spirit alone who does the work of producing the fruit of peace in our lives. We all play a huge role.

In the pressure-packed world we live in, we have struggles and conflicts that seem to occur constantly. We see this in our personal lives, in our careers, and in the communities in which we live. Here we find inconsiderate behavior, insensitivity, unwillingness to get along, manipulation, selfish ambitions, coercion, malice, crime, and all of the acts of the flesh the apostle Paul talks about in his letters. Instead of peace, many would say that much of life is overflowing with stress and conflict.

Yes, there are struggles in almost every human pursuit. We see people have a hard time in their personal lives for many reasons. On a larger scale, we see major disagreements and conflicts between countries leading to all kinds of conflicts and wars. Unfortunately, having troubles, whether we are at fault or not, is a constant in life.

So, how can we have more peace and be effective peacemakers? Continue on!

Definition of Peace

Let's first begin by coming together on terms.
The *Webster's Dictionary* defines peace in the following ways. [59]

a) Freedom from war or a stopping of war
b) Freedom from public disturbance or disorder, i. e. , law and order
c) Freedom from disagreement or quarrels: harmony
d) Absence of mental conflict: serenity
e) An undisturbed state of mind
f) Calm, quiet and tranquility

These are wonderful descriptions of peace from worldly perspective. How great life on earth would be if we had all of these conditions most of the time!

The Greek word the apostle Paul uses for peace in Galatians 5:22 is **eiréné** (εἰρήνη), pronounced i-ray'-nay. [60] Eiréné occurs over eighty times in the New Testament and is rich in meaning. Here we find the spiritual perspective of peace described.

Eiréné reflects a sense of wholeness and completeness, where things work out and get resolved. It refers to a state of tranquility. It means a serenity of the soul and life without inner conflict. It signals the rule of order, which replaces chaos. This word indicates peace between individuals leading to harmony and agreement. It includes a calm and harmonious absence of conflict. Eiréné is a lack of fear and a sense of contentment. It is fellowship and unity between individuals. It is freedom from worry and disturbing thoughts. [61] These are all wonderful concepts!

Of course, we know that the concept of peace is more than the absence of war between nations or a feeling of tranquility in the mind. Its first and most important aspect is in reference to a right relationship with God. What we learn from this process is what can help us facilitate peace within ourselves and with others.

The God of Peace

We know the Scriptures are clear in describing our heavenly Father as a God of peace. Consider the following passages.

- **1 Corinthians 14:33:** For God is not a God of disorder, but of peace.
- **Romans 15:33:** The God of peace be with you all. Amen.
- **Romans 16:20:** The God of peace will soon crush Satan under your feet.
- **2 Corinthians 13:11:** Aim for perfection, listen to my appeal, be of one mind, live in peace. And the God of love and peace will be with you.

From these passages, we understand that peace is closely associated with God. Indeed, it is one of God's encouraging attributes. We know that sin entered the world with Adam and Eve and has flourished ever since. We understand this because our sin, disobedience, and rebellion has once alienated and separated us from God. However, we know that in His foreknowledge, our loving Father made plans to fix this problem from before the world was created. The God of peace brings peace through forgiveness and reconciliation. Through Jesus, the Prince of Peace, God has made a way for us to be reconciled with Him.

What we will find is that peace is a multi-dimensional issue. It's not just about the absence of problems. If it is dependent upon not having problems, then we will never find peace. Peace is about establishing and maintaining a proper relationship with God. It's about doing the same with each other. It's also about finding a way to be at peace within ourselves, being right with ourselves.

So we find that there are three types of peace commonly referred to in the Scriptures.

1. Peace with God;
2. Peace of God (peace within ourselves); and
3. Peace with others (peace between people).

We will spend the rest of this chapter unpacking these three concepts as we explore the dimensions of eiréné.

1. Peace with God

Establishing peace with God is the most important quest in life. It aligns with the purpose of God in creating us in the first place. Peace with God makes a relationship with God possible. Peace with God is our greatest aim. Peace with God is the whole reason Jesus came to earth. The weight and importance of all of this should grab us in the deepest regions of our soul. It deserves to be at the apex of our goals and priorities. Without peace with God, no one can live a meaningful, purposeful life. If one chooses not to pursue peace with God, it can only be seen as a rejection of God. It's the same essence as being an avowed atheist.

Affirming a major theme in how God interacts with us in life, He is the one who takes the initiative in this. He provides the way for peace. We respond. The basis of our peace with God is our justification by faith in Jesus Christ. Jesus came to earth to restore what was broken, our relationship with God, and make it whole again. That's eiréné. That's why Christians are filled with love and gratitude to God for His grace and mercy.

Let's consider the following Scriptures that speak about this.

Romans 5:1–2:

> Therefore, since we have been justified through faith, we have peace with God through our Lord Jesus Christ, through whom we have gained access by faith into this grace in which we now stand. And we boast in the hope of the glory of God.

Peace with God comes to us when we become reconciled to God through the work and grace of Jesus. It is because of what God did through Jesus that we can have peace with Him. This is what provides the hope we have for a home in heaven. Jesus talks about this in the passage below.

John 14:1–4:

> Do not let your hearts be troubled. Trust in God; trust also in me. In my Father's house are many rooms; if it were not so, I would have told you. I am going there to prepare a place for you. And if I go and prepare a place for you, I will come back and take you to be with me that you also may be where I am. You know the way to the place where I am going.

Having peace with God is the foundation for the hope we have for a life with God after we pass on from this life. Also, having peace with God is the basis for having peace within ourselves and peace with other people. This foundation, however, does not guarantee that these other aspects of peace occur automatically. We must pursue and cultivate that which makes for peace.

2. Peace of God (Peace within Ourselves)

When we consider the idea of having peace within ourselves, we must ask two questions: (1) What does this mean? and (2) What does it look like? Having peace with God is the foundation of being able to have peace within ourselves. When we become right with God, we achieve an incredible sense of wholeness and completeness. We are in alignment with our purpose in life. With God, there is no unfinished business.

As followers of Christ, we are called to have an inner peace. However, this is not a simple or easy process. There are many factors at play here. Because of this, it is hard to even define what this kind of peace means and how we experience this in our lives.

Inner peace, or peace within ourselves, relates to factors such as our psychological and emotional well-being/stability as well as the many dimensions of our personal lives, including all of the personal relationships we have with family and friends, our careers, marriage, financial matters, health, and so on. If inner peace is contingent on having all aspects of our personal lives stress-free without any conflicts or challenges, we'll never find peace.

Let's take a look at a passage of Scripture we've examined before, but for another purpose. Let's see what it has to say to us about inner peace.

Philippians 4:4–7:

> Rejoice in the Lord always. I will say it again: Rejoice!
> Let your gentleness be evident to all. The Lord is near.
> Do not be anxious about anything, but in every situation,
> by prayer and petition, with thanksgiving, present your
> requests to God. And the peace of God, which transcends
> all understanding, will guard your hearts and your minds
> in Christ Jesus.

Peace that guards our hearts and minds is a peace that won't let our circumstances get the better of us. Our inner peace comes from our relationship and connection to the Prince of Peace. It is a peace from God through the Holy Spirit that is beyond understanding. So, how do we explain the unexplainable? Worldly logic cannot describe this peace given the spiritual dimensions upon which it is based. It is peace we can have regardless of our circumstances. It is based upon our relationship with God. This peace is possible because we take heart in knowing that Christ has overcome the world. This peace guards our hearts and minds as we stay in close relationship with Christ. This inner personal peace is what makes it possible for us to have joy and the other fruit of the Spirit in Galatians 5:22–23.

We also understand that unbelievers, those not in a relationship with Christ, cannot experience this peace nor is it likely they care to understand it.

The inner peace we have also relates to us being satisfied with the life we are living. The only way this can happen is if we have a clear sense of meaning and purpose. Only those in a reconciled relationship with God can access this meaning and purpose. From God, we are given a new set of guiding beliefs and values which are communicated to us through the Scriptures. All of this enables us to live in ways that are pleasing to us and grateful to God. Therefore, we can have inner peace.

The apostle Paul talks about the peace of Christ in the following passage:

Colossians 3:15–17:

> Let the peace of Christ rule in your hearts, to which indeed you were called in one body; and be thankful. Let the word of Christ richly dwell within you, with all wisdom teaching and admonishing one another with psalms and hymns and spiritual songs, singing with thankfulness in your hearts to God. Whatever you do in word or deed, do all in the name of the Lord Jesus, giving thanks through Him to God the Father.

This passage emphasizes how we receive peace by staying close to Christ. We let His Word dwell richly in us, we sing spiritual songs, and we have thankful hearts. We do all of this in the name of Christ.

The point is, we must not allow our life's circumstances to take away our peace. Yes, that's easier said than done. We need to learn what the apostle Paul learned in being content whatever the circumstances. His life experiences since becoming a follower and apostle of Christ provide a powerful witness to others.

Let's first look at some of the challenging circumstances of the apostle Paul's life as he reviews it in **2 Corinthians 11:23–27:**

> Are they servants of Christ? (I am out of my mind to talk like this.) I am more. I have worked much harder, been in prison more frequently, been flogged more severely, and been exposed to death again and again. Five times I received from the Jews the forty lashes minus one. Three times I

was beaten with rods, once I was pelted with stones, three times I was shipwrecked, I spent a night and a day in the open sea, I have been constantly on the move. I have been in danger from rivers, in danger from bandits, in danger from my fellow Jews, in danger from Gentiles; in danger in the city, in danger in the country, in danger at sea; and in danger from false believers. I have labored and toiled and have often gone without sleep; I have known hunger and thirst and have often gone without food; I have been cold and naked.

So, how can a person who has been through all of that be able to have a life of inner peace? We know it was his faith, a strong relationship with God and his commitment to his mission that kept him going. He was able to cope with his circumstances with joy in his heart. It is possible! The next Scripture gives us clues to how he did it.

Philippians 4:11–13:

I am not saying this because I am in need, for I have learned to be content whatever the circumstances. I know what it is to be in need, and I know what it is to have plenty. I have learned the secret of being content in any and every situation, whether well fed or hungry, whether living in plenty or in want. I can do all this through him who gives me strength.

Yes, this relates to inner peace and strength. How did the apostle Paul learn this? It was through his experiences. This is a process that occurs over time. He is telling us that he was able to live a godly life and experience joy and peace through all the challenges he faced because of what he learned. This experience of contentment comes from looking backward. He learned to lean on God and pray and receive strength from his faith and from the Holy Spirit. He's not just showing off. He's sharing this so it can help us.

Now, if the apostle Paul has to learn things in order to cope with life, so must we. We should not intentionally bypass the learning process expecting the Holy Spirit to do things for us. We must embrace the opportunity to learn many lessons from life. It is experiences in life over time which enables one to make evaluative comments like the apostle Paul has done.

We know the apostle Paul is very humble before God. He is incredibly thankful for the mercy of God as he considers himself the worst of all sinners. Consider what he says about this.

1 Timothy 1:12–17:

> Here is a trustworthy saying that deserves full acceptance: Christ Jesus came into the world to save sinners—of whom I am the worst. But for that very reason I was shown mercy so that in me, the worst of sinners, Christ Jesus might display his immense patience as an example for those who would believe in him and receive eternal life. Now to the King eternal, immortal, invisible, the only God, be honor and glory forever and ever. Amen.

Paul was a persecutor of Christians before he became a Christian (Acts 9). This changed his life dramatically. Paul knew his place before God. He was humble and grateful, never boastful. He never forgot where he came from and how his life has changed because of Christ. His gratitude toward God ran deep and it was ever present. And so can it be for us. Having the hope for eternal life with God through our Savior Jesus Christ is the foundation for our inner peace. What we build upon this foundation can be something very special.

There are many people who believe they have sinned against God terribly and fear that God's mercy and forgiveness will not extend to them. The example above regarding how Paul was forgiven should give us all encouragement and hope. We don't have to fear. If God can forgive Paul, God will also forgive us if we repent, become born again, and then be a faithful follower of Christ.

To be able to have peace within ourselves, we must be able to find inner contentment. Oftentimes, we seem to be harder on ourselves when we make mistakes than we are on other people when they make mistakes. Many are known to be perfectionists. This plays into it. We must realize that we all make mistakes and accept the principle that mistakes are for learning. Thanks to God's grace and mercy, we don't have to be perfect to be acceptable to God.

Yes, we have been released and liberated from the reasons for our guilt and shame. We can approach life with inner peace minus the spiritual baggage from our past. This does not have to weigh us down. This freedom can provide us with emotional strength and propel us to accomplishing great things in life.

Obstacles to Inner Peace

Even though Christians have peace with God, there can remain many disrupters of our inner peace. These can include adversity, anxiety, difficult life situations, failures to living according to our values, and the normal suffering we experience along life's journey. Inner peace can relate to whether we have any regrets or unfinished business in our lives. So yes, there can be many obstacles to come. However, Jesus knew this would be the case.

We understand that having "peace" does not mean we won't have troubles. Jesus told this to His disciples in **John 16:33**:

> I have told you these things, so that in me you may have peace. In this world you will have trouble. But take heart! I have overcome the world.

In the gospel of John, chapters 14–16, Jesus had been in a long discussion with his disciples. This provides the context for this verse. Jesus spoke to them about His leaving, the Holy Spirit coming, Him being the true vine, their need to obey His command to love God and love each other, and then that the world is going to hate them. So yes, they will have troubles. However, Jesus said they can have peace in the midst of the troubles. So can all of us. Yes, in the world we will have trouble, but Jesus has overcome the world. Through Jesus, so do we!

So, how can this be? The answer is, we must be focused on the end. Stephen Covey, in his book, *The 7 Habits of Highly Effective People: Powerful Lessons in Personal Change*, relates to this. From what he learned from his research, effective people were those who were able to "begin with the end in mind."[62] The Scriptures also convey to us that we need to have the end in mind as we endure the joys and trials of life. We need to keep in mind the reward waiting for all of us after we pass on from this life to a home in heaven.

This relates to what Paul said in **Romans 8:18**:

> I consider that our present sufferings are not worth comparing with the glory that will be revealed in us.

Paul is saying that our future inheritance, our hope for a home in heaven, vastly outweighs our present sufferings, and this should help us cope with our adversities and lead to inner peace.

This relates to what James said in **James 1:12**:

> Blessed is the man who perseveres under trial, because when he has stood the test, he will receive the crown of life that God has promised to those who love him.

The Scriptures tell us to look forward to the final judgment as a decisive answer from God to human suffering. It will be our crown of life.

Now, this is not to minimize the significance and challenge personal problems can play in our lives. We should all seek to resolve these as much as we can. If one gets stuck and can't seem to progress, then seeking help is the way to go. For the less complicated issues, this help can come from loving family members and trusted friends. For many others, this will not be enough. I'm certainly a believer in the effectiveness of Christian professional counseling. Everyone should be committed to doing what they can to find inner peace.

When I think of good people around us who are not Christians, I have to wonder from where they can find inner peace. These are people who have not found or accepted the truth about God and the eternal salvation that is only available in Jesus Christ. These are people who must be good at denial and an ability to keep things spiritual out of their minds. Any true inner peace is not available to them. For whatever reason, it certainly seems that most of them are very stubborn in their view that spiritual matters are not important.

Here are a few questions for these people to ponder.

- What are the origins of creation?
- What is their basis for morality?
- From where do they get their purpose for living?
- What is their destiny after life?

3. Peace with Others

Having peace with others rounds out and completes the circle of peace we must have to be able to have the peace the apostle Paul refers to in Galatians 5:22. We know there are many Scriptures that appeal to us to live at peace with others. Let's review some of these passages.

Romans 14:19:

Make every effort to do what leads to peace.

The Greek word for "make every effort" is the word **diókó** (διώκω), pronounced dee-o'-ko. [63] The word means to aggressively chase, like a hunter pursuing a catch (prize). It means to pursue with all haste, earnestly desiring to overtake (apprehend).

Hebrews 12:14:

Make every effort to live in peace with all men...

Paul says in **Romans 12:18:**

If it is possible, as far as it depends on you, live at peace with everyone.

"As far as it depends on you..." This is an admonition that applies many times where the Scriptures tell us to do things.

Jesus says in **Matthew 5:9**, what we call the beatitudes, the following:

Blessed are the peacemakers, for they will be called sons of God.

The Greek word for peacemaking is **eirénopoios** (εἰρηνοποιός), which is pronounced i-ray-nop-oy-os. [64] This refers to the idea of loving peace and being a peacemaker, a peace-pursuer. All of the above passages convey the importance and urgency for attaining peace. Without peace, what would life and relationships look like?

Pursue Healthy Relationships

In a practical sense, having peace with others and having peace with God is all about having quality, appropriate, and healthy relationships. This relates to relationships in all aspects of life. Does this come easily and naturally? Unfortunately, no! Having quality and meaningful relationships takes concerted effort. All of this should be characterized by the following concepts and personal actions:

- Pursue effective communication, listening well, understanding each other's thoughts, feelings, and needs, not interrupting others, and so on.
- Seek to understand a person before expecting them to understand you, putting them first.
- Avoid words and attitudes that create hurt feelings.
- Avoid jumping to conclusions, which can create unnecessary conflict.
- Practice effective problem-solving skills and be proactive in addressing and resolving conflicts at the time they occur. Don't wait to deal with these. This can enable them to become even larger issues.
- Don't seek revenge or retaliation.
- Have the sincere agape kind of love toward others and a heart of compassion.
- Be quick to apologize when in the wrong.
- Forgive others and seek to restore relationships when possible. Don't hold grudges.
- Treat others honorably and respectfully.
- Be trustworthy, dependable, and honest.
- Be emotionally stable and rational in behavior and attitudes.

Now, this is a good start for a list of how we can have healthy relationships with others. Can you see how doing all of these things can facilitate peace with others?

Conflict Resolution

One of the major reasons why we don't have peace with others is because of the many conflicts we have with them. Many of these come our way because others create the issues. Sometimes we do. Some of these can involve complex situations, such as deep and long-standing issues between people that have never been resolved. Some come our way that are minor in intensity and more simple and easy to resolve.

Much of how we deal with conflict has its roots in our families, how we were taught to handle conflict. Those in healthy families have learned constructive ways to deal with harmful issues, such as confronting them quickly when they are small and using good communication and problem-solving skills to resolve them. For those who were raised in dysfunctional families, how they were taught to handle conflicts often include dysfunctional approaches of aggression, avoidance, overreacting, withdrawing, and so on.

The Range of Ways We Handle Conflict

The following list captures many of the ways people choose to handle a conflict. Only one way is the constructive and healthy way.

1. To avoid the situation and stay clear of conflict.
2. To win at all costs, be very competitive and aggressive and go for the jugular.
3. To give in and pursue peace at any price.
4. To hold things in and then explode.
5. To be passive-aggressive which means being aggressive by passive means.
6. To not confront the situation directly but indirectly handle it by acting better toward the person as a way to makeup for the trouble one has caused.
7. To be assertive, confront the situation with gentleness, and seek to resolve issues on a timely basis. (This is the best way!)

Factors in Problem-Solving

The following is my rendition of a problem-solving model that can help resolve issues between two people. This procedure is best done together in a discussion with the person with whom a conflict exists.

1. Stay calm at all times.
2. Define the problem.
3. Acknowledge who owns the problem the most. *(Who is the situation impacting the most? Who is raising the issue or making the complaint? Whose goals are being blocked by the problem?)*
4. Identify how each person contributes to the problem.
5. Identify underlying issues related to the problem.
6. Understand how the past influences the problem.
7. Understand the function of the problem. What is its purpose?
8. Agree to work toward resolution of the problem.
9. Generate possible solutions to the problem.
10. Evaluate each alternative solution.
11. Select the best solution.
12. Implement the solution.
13. Evaluate your progress. If it isn't working, try something else.

The Communication Process for Conflicts

Effective communication is essential if conflicts are to be resolved in a constructive and loving way. Unfortunately, relationships characterized by serious conflict often have been enduring along-standing pattern of problems. Poor or ineffective communication is one of the common reasons why. Not getting issues resolved, especially in timely manner, is another major reason why resolution is not found. These two reasons go together.

I have often found in marriage counseling that I needed to first educate and train couples on good communication techniques. Again, these were often noticeably absent in their relationship. This was especially true for couples who argue quite a bit and forcefully. I believe learning effective communication techniques needs to occur before issues can be effectively addressed.

One of the techniques I have used in helping couples improve their communication, especially for those in highly troubled relationships, is to have them use a specific communication process. This is my version of the active listening technique. I ask couples to stick strictly to the process. I have found that this has worked wonders for those who will use it effectively.

The communication process goes like this:

1. Decide who will begin first to share their point of view. You will take turns with this.
2. Share your point of view. Do this in "bite size" portions.
3. Stop after a short while and ask the listener to reflect back what you have said. For the listener/reflector, do not add to it. The task is just to mirror back what the other person said. Use the same words. Do not make conclusions, give an opinion, or defend yourself at this stage. No "buts"...
4. After the reflection, ask if you missed anything. If you have, the other person will restate it, and you are then to reflect it back.
5. The listener then reflects back the emotions he or she sees underneath the content. The other person can validate this observation or explain it another way, if desired.
6. Then, do your best to validate the merits of the person's point of view. What is good about it? How is it logical and sound? Empathize with the person. See things from their perspective. How can you agree with their point of view? Join with their feelings!

Then repeat the process with the other person sharing their perspective on what is going on. Keep repeating this process for the full discussion.

Now, this process should only be used with major issues. I have found that this is a difficult process to learn and execute well. However, once learned, it can make a huge difference in improving a couples' communication and for strengthening their relationship.

Conclusion

Presented in this chapter are scriptural insights on how to cultivate peace in the major areas of our lives. Also offered are some practical suggestions on how to have healthy relationships which are the best context for peace. God has called Christians to be peacemakers. We must experience peace in order to be able to facilitate peace in the lives of others.

We see that God is the source of peace between Himself and mankind. God is the one who determines what peace is and the requirements of peace. God can also be in the middle of all peace efforts, including the peace we can have within ourselves and with others. We know what God does is linked to His attributes. The God of peace is the maker of peace and the giver of peace. There is no true and lasting peace outside of Him. Because God is peace, He wants His people to be like Him. He wants us to be peacemakers.

If you are one who is not experiencing peace, consider the causes. Remember, we all have our blind spots. It might be helpful to seek assistance from a Christian professional counselor if the situation is serious. It might be helpful to seek pastoral counseling to deal with issues between you and God.

CHAPTER 6

Patience

A Precious Gift to Those We Love

> "Be completely humble and gentle; be patient, bearing
> with one another in love."

—Ephesians 4:2

We now come to patience, the fourth "fruit of the Spirit" mentioned in Galatians 5:22–23. Patience may be seen as a virtue, but it is often an elusive one. Most of us live in a cultural context that is overwhelmed by people in a hurry. Some have labeled it as "hurry sickness."[65] It's described as a continual struggle to accomplish more things and participate in more events in less time. Many get upset if others don't drive fast enough, when the grocery lines are too slow, and when wait times are too long at all kinds of appointments. When we create more stress in our lives, we are likely to make more mistakes.

Most everyone will admit they struggle regularly with having patience. Many seem to speak about this personal weakness in lighthearted ways as if it is no big deal. I wonder if many underestimate the importance of patience in our lives. I just think this is an area in which we all can make great improvements if we will honor our loved ones more and make a commitment to work harder on developing this quality in our lives.

In preparing my thoughts for this chapter, I watched several YouTube sermons on patience from several preachers representing differing theological orientations. All of them admitted they personally struggled with having patience. Now, some may see this as being a little hypocritical. After all, shouldn't preachers "practice what they preach" to be authentic and genuine? In light of this and other common deficiencies, one preacher claimed rights to the following maxim: "My right to teach the gospel is not dependent on my ability to practice it perfectly." I'm pretty sure all of us are sympathetic with that sentiment.

Patience Defined

Webster's Definition

The *Webster's Dictionary* defines patience as bearing or enduring pain and trouble without complaining or losing self-control. Patience involves the bearing of suffering, provocation, delay, tediousness, and so on with calmness and self-control. [66]

We understand patience to mean the ability to endure whatever opposition and frustrations come our way and to show perseverance without wanting retaliation or revenge. Patience is slowness in avenging wrongs. It is the quality of restraint that prevents Christian believers from speaking or acting hastily in the face of frustration, disagreement, or opposition. Patience enables the bearing of irritations or problems without complaining.

Greek Word for Patience

The Greek word for patience in Galatians 5:22, and the most commonly used word for patience in the New Testament, is "**makrothumia**" (μακροθυμία). [67] It is pronounced mak-roth-oo-meh'-ah. It means to suffer long (long-suffering), having patience, being tolerant, and having perseverance. It relates to being long-tempered, which leads to waiting sufficient time before getting angry. This avoids the premature use of force and retribution that rises out of improper anger.

We can see from these definitions that God wants us to be slow to get angry and slow to lash out at people. We need to develop a long fuse and be able to patiently handle the provocations that come our way. Christians must be better at handling these kinds of irritations.

Outline for Chapter

We'll proceed through this chapter using the following outline to discuss this important topic: (1) the patience of God, (2) patience with others, (3) love is patient, and (4) impatience and anger.

1. The Patience of God

Yes, God does get impatient and angry at times. But He does so in righteous and appropriate ways. We understand this fits within the realm of righteous indignation. As a godly character issue, the Scriptures talk about God being slow to anger to reflect His loving and kind heart toward people. Consider the following passages.

Exodus 34:6:

> And he [God] passed in front of Moses, proclaiming, "The Lord, the Lord, the compassionate and gracious God, slow to anger, abounding in love and faithfulness..."

Psalm 103:8:

> The Lord is compassionate and gracious, slow to anger, abounding in love.

Romans 2:4:

> Or do you show contempt for the riches of His kindness, tolerance and patience, not realizing that God's kindness leads you toward repentance.

1 Timothy 1:15–16:

> Here is a trustworthy saying that deserves full acceptance: Christ Jesus came into the world to save sinners—of whom I am the worst. But for that very reason I was shown mercy so that in me, the worst of sinners, Christ might display

his unlimited patience as an example for those who would believe on him and receive eternal life.

James 5:11:

The Lord is full of compassion and mercy.

Yes, God has amazing qualities. All of these reflect His holiness, perfection, and love. Many of these are essential for tolerating and embracing human beings who can be extremely fickle and inconsistent in doing what is right and unable to maintain a close relationship with Him. We all must take great comfort knowing that God is rich in kindness, tolerance, patience, grace, compassion, and mercy.

2. Patience with Others

There are many Scriptures that appeal to Christians to be patient. This relates to a concept we've been highlighting all throughout this book: God wants us to be like Him. Patience is another one of the character traits of God. Therefore, the Scriptures underscore how God wants us to be patient and slow to anger. Consider the following passages.

Colossians 3:12: Clothe yourselves with... patience.

James 5:7: "Be patient, then brothers, until the Lord's coming."

Proverbs 14:29: "A patient man has great understanding, but a quick-tempered man displays folly."

Colossians 1:10: "And we pray this in order that you may live a life worthy of the Lord and please him in every way..."

Yes, patience is a virtue. It is an ability that all people can learn with constant nurturing. It comes from a disciplined life. It is within everyone's grasp. Social scientists who study patience are finding that patience is one of the keys to a happy life. Patient people tend to experience less depression and negative emotions. They are more cooperative, empathic, and forgiving.

Patience provides the time we need to assess situations and consider how we can best respond. Patience allows us the time to make better decisions. [68]

Most people would say that impatience is a huge problem in our world today. Frustration and impatience do not lead to positive outcomes. Quite the contrary, the outcomes from impatient encounters are often discouragement, hurt feelings, and damaged relationships.

Living in a close and intimate relationship with impatient people can be a real struggle. Some people, for the sake of peace, just do not push back and let the impatient person mistreat them. Others, in an effort to stand up to an impatient spouse, learn to develop similar aggressive behaviors in order to defend themselves. However, this often does not lead to issues getting resolved. In fact, what we see is more arguing and fighting going on. All of those who can find the strength should gently yet firmly confront impatient persons and demand that they treat them with more love and respect. This poor treatment often coincides with situations where impatient spouses have more power in the relationship.

The Civil Rights Movement has shown that power concedes nothing without a demand. Applying this to unequal power in marital relationships, the weaker spouse must find ways to make assertive demands for being treated properly. This requires having the self-esteem and self-confidence to confront the other spouse.

The key to being patient is self-awareness and self-control. Often, impatient people don't realize they are being impatient nor do they see it as a problem in a relationship. Impatient people would do well to give others permission to point out to them when this happens in a problematic way. They then need to accept this insight and express gratitude to the other person when it is given to them. We all need to understand that patience can save us from many regrets.

Titus 2:11–12:

> For the grace of God has appeared that offers salvation to all people. It teaches us to say "No" to ungodliness and worldly passions, and to live self-controlled, upright and godly lives in this present age...

What do we like about patient people?

1. They are pleasant to be around.
2. They are welcoming and endearing.
3. They are easy to get along with as we interact with them.
4. They are respectful, kind, and loving people.
5. They value us and make us feel respected and important.
6. They are better at reading situations and solving problems.

How do we feel about being around impatient people?

1. Their prickliness is uncomfortable to be around. We'd rather avoid impatient people.
2. We become hurt and offended if the impatience is aimed at us.
3. It's like we have to walk on egg shells around those who are prone to be impatient so as not to get them upset.
4. Being the brunt of enduring impatience over time can negatively impact the feelings we have toward that person.

3. Love Is Patient

We read in 1 Corinthians 13:4 that love is patient. Being patient is one of the behavioral ways to say "I love you" to others. This captures a lot of truth about patience! Being patient says a loved one is important to us. It says we value a loved one and our relationship with him or her. Having patience forces us to be thoughtful and breaks the habit of being self-centered and selfish. Being patient is a way to show we care deeply about another person and their feelings. Being patient with others will draw people closer together.

On the other hand, being impatient is a way to assert, "I am more important than you." It says my needs are more important than your needs. It claims, "I can do what I want no matter what you think, and I don't care how my behavior impacts you." Being impatient pushes people away from each other. Impatience is poison to a relationship.

In reality, patience is a precious gift we give to those we love. It is like a bright, shining jewel. It is one of the big ways we show others how important they are to us. It is a sign of true love and respect. Just ask your spouse how they feel when you are patient with them. Then ask them how they feel when you are impatient with them.

We all need to learn to be more patient. Everyone we interact with will thank us. Again, the truth is, nobody enjoys being around impatient people.

Being on the receiving end of a person's impatience can cause emotional stress, discouragement, and damages one's self-esteem. There are no positive outcomes to being the brunt of unwarranted, harsh, and inconsiderate behavior from another.

Some Reasons Why People Become Impatient

1. They are too busy, under time pressures, and stressed out.
2. They are in a hurry and have to rush.
3. They are in a bad mood.
4. They are not a very happy person. They don't have much joy in their life.
5. The get frustrated about things that one expects should go better, such as unfulfilled expectations.
6. They are not a very loving person.
7. They have insecurities and lash out because of lower self-esteem issues.
8. They are not a strong person spiritually.
9. They may continue to be impatient deliberately in order to intimidate others and get their way.

Why don't you discuss the above with your spouse, if applicable? Can we see that the responses above are things a person can improve upon with greater self-awareness, self-control, a better way of thinking, and with better problem-solving skills? Can we understand that people may have to change their behavior and attitudes in response to frustrating situations in order to prevent impatience? Sometimes people get impatient because they are having a bad and stressful day. This is causing them to be in a bad mood. In such cases, this person should warn their spouse they are in a bad mood so the spouse can give them space and time to regroup. If impatience comes from insecurities and lower self-esteem issues, then seeking professional counseling may be the best solution.

As we see a distinct emphasis in the Scriptures on being patient, we can certainly appreciate that there are many good reasons for it!

Suggestions for Improving Your Impatience Problem

1. First, accept you have a problem with being patient and make a commitment to improving this weakness in your life.
2. Realize that impatience is a major problem, not a minor irritation.
3. Recognize your motivation for working on the issue. Write down specific reasons why you need to take the journey to improvement, which include the benefits of being patient.
4. Be aware of what provokes your impatient actions, the buttons that get pushed that cause it. Focus on yourself as you assign causes and blame.
5. Develop more healthy habits of the mind in response to the provocations in life.
6. Repent of your harsh and impatient ways.
7. Pray for help and strength to fight this personal battle.
8. Understand you have your blind spots. You may not even know when you are being impatient. It would be helpful if you could find those who can help you recognize when this is occurring.
9. Evaluate yourself at the end of every day to review how patient you were. Specifically:
   a. What impatient incident happened?
   b. How could you have handled the situation better?
10. Realize that improvement is a process. There will be ups and downs. Do not get discouragesd if it is taking longer than you expected.

One important consideration in the process of making improvements in our lives is that we are human beings with inherent limitations. It's best to consider growth and improvement as never totally arriving. We don't "master" issues like this one. We always have to take it a day at a time. It's not that we achieve success and, therefore, can move on and won't be vulnerable to this issue again.

4. Impatience and Anger

I believe it's worth noting that impatience and anger are in the same family of reactions. The impact of impatience on others is similar to the impact of anger on others. The difference is a matter of degree and intensity.

As with impatience, most people do not like to be around angry people for the same reasons. Impatience and anger are both bad habits of the mind.

Anger is often, if not always, a secondary emotion. This means that anger has its roots in something that is going on underneath the surface. Take away anger and see what is left.

A profound Scripture about anger is found in **James 1:19–20**:

> My dear brothers and sisters, take note of this: Everyone should be quick to listen, slow to speak and slow to become angry, because human anger does not produce the righteousness that God desires.

The same admonition could be said about impatience. Human impatience does not produce the righteousness that God desires. The problem is people are often slow to listen, quick to speak, and quick to become angry. Most would agree that although there is often a strong urge to respond with anger in provocative situations, this just makes the situation worse. Many have said that reacting with anger is like pouring gasoline on a fire that is already blazing. A chemical retardant would be far better.

Is the response of anger a choice we make? Is anger subject to our self-control? How many times have you seen others try to minimize the impact of, or responsibility for, their anger? They may say something like, "That's just the way I am, and you have to accept me." How many times do you see people admit their weakness but never improve? They may say, "I know I need to control my anger," but they never do learn to control it. Then there are those who shift responsibility and blame others for their anger and often say, "You made me angry."

There are many reasons and excuses why people continue in their lack of anger control. Some people are just undisciplined and impulsive. Sometimes anger reactions are used as smoke screens to hide how a person really feels. Some anger reactions can be used to deflect attention away from immediate issues in order to avoid them. Some people deliberately continue in anger because they know it intimidates others, and they use this as a manipulation ploy to get what they want.

Unfortunately, everyone else has to pay the price for the privilege the impatient and angry persons claim for themselves as they continue with their behavior. This results in relationships becoming strained and forces people to develop habits of avoidance. It could also result in habits of retribution toward the aggressor.

One of the realities regarding anger is that it can be accompanied by physical reactions. One of these is known as the "fight or flight" response. As people get charged up with anger, adrenaline is pumped into the bloodstream, which sets off a series of physiological responses. Blood pressure increases. Blood-containing needed nourishment circulates more rapidly throughout the body. The pupils of the eyes dilate for better peripheral vision. The hands get sweaty, and the mouth gets dry. The muscles tense up and are supplied with additional energy. The digestive tract can become so spastic that severe pains are felt during and after the time one is angry.

Certainly, this response does not occur every time a person is angry, but you can particularly notice it with the more intense feelings of anger. This is understood as an involuntary physiological response that occurs whether or not we wish it to happen.

God has created this system as a means by which the body can protect itself against danger. I don't believe He would reprimand us for anger's proper functioning. However, I believe there are times when we can avert this "fight or flight" response by not letting ourselves become so charged up in provocative circumstances. Again, self-control is the remedy. We should also pray for God to give us strength in this area.

When Is Anger a Problem?

How do you know when anger is a problem? What would you say? Sometimes people are blind to this reality. It can be likened to a common defensive response from alcoholics: "I'm not as bad as so and so." Well, there are many indicators reflecting the reality that anger is a problem. Some of these would be when it is too frequent, when it is too intense, when it lasts too long, and when it leads to aggression. You also know you have a problem when people avoid you. Any one of these conditions is a cause for great concern.

One of the questions I know many people struggle with is whether anger is a sin. I believe we need not look very far to answer that question. We all know that both God and Jesus experienced anger. In fact, the Old Testament has over 375 references to the anger and wrath of God. There are also several references to the anger of Jesus in the New Testament.

The classic Scripture often used to answer this question is Ephesians 4:26, where Paul states, "In your anger, do not sin." It would certainly appear that the exercise of the will stands in the gap between the two halves of that verse. In the first half, "in your anger," we then should think, be alert, and watch ourselves. This is so that in the second half, we "do not sin." A common understanding of this Scripture is that it is not the anger itself that is wrong, but that anger has the potential for leading us into sin. When we are angry, we are more vulnerable to sin. This can easily occur when we convert our angry feelings into aggressive or hostile actions.

Some Helpful Suggestions in Dealing with Anger

- Pray for those who hurt us and irritate us. Praying for people helps us have a better perspective and attitude toward them.
- Forgive others who have wronged us. This includes releasing them from any claims we have against them. It involves giving up our need to hurt back.
- Focus on positive attitudes and become more spiritually oriented in our lives.
- Understand our responsibility for our anger and not shift the blame on to others.
- Develop habits of self-control where we slow our reactions and think before we respond.
- Look at the sources of our anger and deal constructively with these. If you take away anger, what then would be the issue? Then deal with the issue.
- For some, it may be good to get professional counseling to overcome this problem. This is most indicated when anger is a long-lasting issue in your life and you've tried but have been unsuccessful in defeating this problem.

Conclusion

I hope the case has been made that patience is an incredibly important quality. On the other hand, I hope the case has also been made very clearly that impatience is a major problem in personal and business relationships. I would think most people want to be liked by others. I would think that most people don't want to hurt or mistreat others. There are numerous reasons to be motivated to become more patient. Understanding all of this can help us do what it takes to be more patient.

For those who struggle substantially with impatience, would one of the reasons be that they want to be impatient and alienate themselves from others? Do people enjoy being impatient? For most, the answer to those two questions is absolutely no. So why, then, do impatient people remain this way? I'm certain there are many reasons, but let's stipulate that it's not because it's always deliberate and intentional. I think much of continuing impatient behavior has to be based on a lack of self-awareness, a lack of self-motivation, and a lack of self-control.

We've addressed how people can deal with their impatience and anger issues in this chapter. It's time now to put all of this into practice. We all can improve how patient we are, especially toward those closest to us. Patience is the loving and respectful way to act toward others. If you need some extra help to make improvement, please find ways to seek this out. Those with significant impatience have an urgent need to improve.

CHAPTER 7

Kindness

Making Life Easier and Better for Others

Kindness. It costs nothing, but means everything.

—Baz Gale

We now come to kindness, the fifth "fruit of the Spirit" mentioned by the apostle Paul in Galatians 5:22–23. Kindness seems to be a fairly simple concept that everyone can understand. However, being kind God's way can be incredibly challenging at times. Also, we all can likely admit that we could be more kind to others. We'll address this and more in this chapter.

The Importance of Kindness

One way to begin a discussion on the concept of kindness is to acknowledge its importance and power. The case for how important kindness is in our lives and in the world is easy to make. We have already acknowledged that kindness is a concept used to define the agape kind of love in 1 Corinthians 13:4. That alone underscores its importance!

As we progress through this chapter, we will understand more clearly the great power of kindness. The reality is, as we show kindness and make kindness a way of life, there are benefits and blessings for those who receive kindness and for those who give kindness.

As I was researching this topic, I came across some studies revealing that we in America are becoming an increasingly rude society. [69] One poll taken several years ago reported that 69 percent of 1,000 adults surveyed said that people are ruder today than they were twenty years ago. Another study revealed that 79 percent of 2,000 adults surveyed described a lack of courtesy in America as being a "serious" problem. Some of the rude behaviors that bothered people were inconsiderate and aggressive driving, poor customer service, inconsiderate cell phone use, and coarse language. We all know there are many more items that could be added to that list.

Even though this may be the case in those studies, I don't think this is a full and complete picture. I believe there is a great deal of kindness being expressed all around us every day, most of the time in ways we are not even aware. In fact, studies investigating kindness are now suggesting we are hardwired for kindness. [70] I believe this could relate to how God made us when he created mankind in His image.

We all witnessed in recent years the response of our country to several major disasters. Hurricane Katrina was one in 2005. I would venture to say that there was hardly a church in America that did not respond to help those who were affected by that natural disaster. We also remember the kind and generous response our country gave to those affected by the terrorist attacks of September 11, 2001, and to the devastating tsunami that hit the Indian Ocean in 2004. We've seen devastating wildfires in California and flooding in Texas due to hurricanes in recent years in which many Americans gave of their money and time to help. And of course, I also think of the generous support that comes to help nonprofit organizations each year. These agencies do tremendous work helping all kinds of people in need. They are a testimony, indeed, of our compassion and kindness!

So yes, even though some studies may reveal that there is a great deal of rudeness in America, overall, I believe there is a much greater amount of kindness in America. Studies investigating this should be more widespread in their focus.

Charles's Story

Many years ago, my brother-in-law, Charles, was stricken with a serious degenerative neurological disorder that affected his brain function. He knew this was a very serious disease that would take his life in a matter of a few years. As the course of that disease progressed, his vision and balance were increasingly affected. He was a devoted jogger and continued to try to keep this routine in his life for as long as he could. In fact, he had a personal goal of trying to jog each and every day. His ability to do this was amazing. Each jog he ran was a personal victory for him.

My sister told me of a time when he was jogging by himself and lost his balance and fell on a sidewalk in front of a dentist's office. The dentist inside happened to see Charles fall down and ran out to help him. The dentist then personally drove him home, knowing that he was hurt and disoriented. This act of kindness touched Charles and my sister very much.

That story is just one example of the many acts of kindness that are occurring around us all the time.

God Is Kind

As we've been acknowledging, God's nature is revealed all throughout the Scriptures. There are many passages relating to God's love, kindness, grace, mercy, patience, and so on.

The apostle Paul refers to the riches of God's kindness in **Romans 2:4**:

> Or do you think lightly of the riches of his kindness and tolerance and patience, not knowing that the kindness of God leads you to repentance?

The riches of God's kindness... something we should value as having priceless worth! How is that possible? By realizing how much our home in heaven means to us. Reminding people of God's kindness could be a helpful way of reaching people for the Lord.

In **Luke 6:35–36**, Jesus challenges us to love and treat all people with love, kindness, and mercy, even our enemies.

> But love your enemies, do good to them, and lend to them without expecting to get anything back. Then your reward will be great, and you will be children of the Most High, because he is kind to the ungrateful and wicked. Be merciful, just as your Father is merciful.

Loving our enemies and doing good to them is quite the opposite of what most people in Jesus's day would think about doing. This is certainly not a natural act. It basically means we can't treat our enemies as enemies. We certainly know Jesus had enemies, some worse than others. We also know that Jesus went to the cross for His enemies. We read in Romans 5:10: "For if, when we were God's enemies, we were reconciled to him through the death of his Son, how much more, having been reconciled, shall we be saved through his life."

Loving our enemies is likely one of the most challenging tasks we've been asked to do. Doing good to them goes against our human instincts. But this is God's way. He is kind to the ungrateful and wicked. That is part of the description of mercy. Mercy is kindness in excess of what may be expected. **Grace** is seen as "getting something you don't deserve" while **mercy** is seen as "not getting something you do deserve." All of this reflects how great and wonderful God is toward people. As His children, God wants us to be like Him in these unique and amazing ways.

The apostle Paul says in **Titus 3:4–5**:

> But when the kindness and love of God our Savior appeared,
> he saved us not because of righteous things we had done,
> but because of his mercy.

As we see, kindness often appears with other adjectives, such as love, mercy, and goodness. These are all words with tremendous and challenging meanings.

Defining Kindness

Yes, we know that kindness is very important in our everyday lives. We also know it is very important to the Lord.

First, let's look at the Greek word used for kindness in Galatians 5:22. It is "**Chrēstotēs**" (χρηστότης), pronounced khray-stot-ace. [71] This refers to being useful and pleasant. The word describes gentleness, goodness, uprightness, generosity, and graciousness. We can see it has broad application. Kindness describes a sympathy that puts others at ease. It is grace and gentleness that pervades the whole nature of a person, mellowing and softening all that might be harsh.

Kindness is always associated with action. Kindness is initiated from a sympathetic and tenderhearted mindset motivated by a loving heart. Kindness is an eagerness to engage with others. It is a sweet and attractive temperament. Kindness is choosing to be sensitive, supportive, gentle, and compassionate to everyone we meet. In a practical sense, kindness means making life easier for people. Kindness goes out looking, wondering, and asking: Who needs some help today? How can I help someone in need? How can I ease someone's burden?

As we noticed earlier, we read in **1 Corinthians 13:4,** where the apostle Paul states that "love is kind." (If God is love, then God is kind.) Kindness is one of the descriptors of love, a close relative to love, if you will. It is an outgrowth and fruit of love. Love and kindness are linked together. Kindness is love in action. Love is what facilitates our connections with others and strengthens our relationships as we show kindness, compassion, and forgiveness to others.

Additional Scriptures on Kindness

As we know, the Scriptures clearly state that kindness is to be one of the qualities that should characterize us as Christians. As a fruit of the Spirit, God wants kindness to be a part of our "spiritual DNA."

The apostle Paul tells us the following in **Ephesians 4:32:**

> Be kind and compassionate to one another, forgiving each other, just as in Christ, God forgave you.

We certainly know that forgiveness is a kind and gracious act on our part. Forgiving another is something we do for those who hurt us, sometimes in malicious and hateful ways. It is not an easy thing to do most of the time. Paul says in **Colossians 3:12–14:**

> Therefore, as God's chosen people, holy and dearly loved, clothe yourselves with compassion, kindness, gentleness and patience. Bear with each other and forgive whatever grievances you may have against one another. Forgive as the Lord forgave you. And over all these virtues put on love, which binds them all together in perfect unity.

The above Scripture uses figurative language to emphasize the importance of several qualities: compassion, kindness, gentleness, and patience. Some have called this our Christian attire. Figuratively, all of these qualities are clothes we are to wear at all times and never take off. In other words, we are to "wear" kindness and compassion when we are under stress, when we are around unkind people, and when we are in difficult circumstances. I think Paul is saying that these qualities should reside deep within us and be visibly displayed regularly and consistently in our lives through our behaviors and actions. What the apostle Paul is encouraging us to do in the above passage is again very challenging to do. Christians are to be different than other people in the world. This difference is to be seen in how we display unnatural acts of love and mercy to others.

2 Peter 1:5–9:

> For this very reason, make every effort to add to your faith, goodness; and to goodness, knowledge; and to knowledge, self-control; and to self-control, perseverance; and to perseverance, godliness; and to godliness, brotherly kindness; and to brotherly kindness, love. For if you possess these qualities in increasing measure, they will keep you from being ineffective and unproductive in your knowledge of our Lord Jesus Christ. But whoever does not have them is nearsighted and blind, forgetting that they have been cleansed from their past sins.

How is it that those who do not have the qualities mentioned in the above passage are considered nearsighted and blind? It is much harder to be effective and productive when one is disabled in those ways. The importance of these qualities is so obvious. These qualities are central to living an authentic Christian life. They are mentioned over and over again. To not possess these qualities reflects those who have lost their passion for the Lord. They don't appreciate the value of being forgiven of their sins and accepted into a reconciled relationship with God. One of our biggest motivators for being kind and doing good deeds to others comes from the gratitude we have toward God for the great things we have received from Him and will continue to receive. Gratitude keeps us aware of His mercy, grace, forgiveness, and reconciliation. Yes, gratitude provides us with strong motivation to respond to do what God wants from us.

Micah 6:8:

> He has shown you, O mortal, what is good. And what does the Lord require of you? To act justly and to love kindness and to walk humbly with your God.

Here, drawing from a prophet of old, we are clearly being told that God wants us to treat others fairly and do what is right. He wants us to be loving and kind people. God wants us to realize who He is and walk humbly with Him. There is no room for arrogant and inconsiderate treatment of others as we pursue a relationship with God. To love kindness suggests that we do reflect this character trait of God in our hearts.

Additional Thoughts on Kindness

The following are insights gained by quotes and sayings. These can help us understand the deeper nature of kindness.

- **Kindness is the root of all good things.** [72] Kindness comes from a heart that cares about other's well-being. It's really about love. Good and kind things come from love.
- **Choose being kind over being right, and you'll be right every time.** [73] Sometimes being right can conflict with being kind. Sometimes being right is not all that important. Many an argument occurs about disagreements that can lead to hurt feelings. They can even create long-term damage to relationships. Being kind includes efforts not to argue much or at least finding more gentle ways to discuss disagreements. It is possible and, in fact, it is not that hard to do. This relates to using effective communication skills.
- **The smallest act of kindness is worth more than the grandest intention.** [74] Best intentions are pretty meaningless without actions and results. Kindness is seen by the actions done. Positive results achieved are the ones that make an impact.
- **What wisdom can you find that is greater than kindness?** [75] Being kind is the right thing to do in most cases. There is wisdom in being

kind. When someone is in need, they don't care how wise one may be. They care about the help given. A wise and loving person will find creative ways to positively impact lives.

The "Faces" of Kindness

As we understand kindness, we see there are many different "faces" or expressions of kindness. We know that kindness is demonstrated in the things we do to make life easier and better for others. Kindness can come in the small things we do for others, like opening a door for someone, or the big things we do, like being a foster parent to abused and neglected children.

Kindness is expressed in what we do for others and what we say to others. Kindness is also expressed by what we do not say or do not do to others. This reflects how we control our impulses. For example, not criticizing, being harsh, or causing embarrassment when people make a mistake can be an example of a kind gesture. Sometimes we express kindness by saying and doing nothing.

We also know there can be a soft and hard side to kindness just as there is a soft and hard side to love. Being kind to a person may mean we need to be firm and assertive at times, such as lovingly confronting friends when they are being unkind or sticking up for someone who is being mistreated by another.

As Robert Strand states in his book, *Kindness*, that quick action is often best when there is an immediate need for kindness. [76] He questions the usefulness of kindness if we do it a day too late. Sometimes, the windows of opportunity are brief. Timing can be a key variable regarding our prospects for making a difference. Ralph Waldo Emerson has said, "You cannot do a kindness too soon, for you never know how soon it will be too late."[77]

The Power of Kindness

As we think about the power of kindness, we understand that kindness can have a great deal of influence in our lives and world. We could not even imagine what the world would be like if people were not kind to each other. It would not be a pleasant place.

True or false: we all depend on kindness. Yes, this is very true! Kindness enables us to cope with life's pressures and brings comfort and assistance at times when it is needed most. It makes a difference every day and enables many to survive in our troubled world. Kindness can facilitate the mending of a broken heart. It can be the exact agent needed for emotional healing. In many ways, kindness is essential. Everyone should do what they can to insert kindness into our world as often as possible.

Mother Teresa once said, "Kind words can be short and easy to speak, but their echoes are truly endless."[78] The impact of being shown kindness can stick with us. Kindness can be endless as we all pass its effects on to others. Mark Twain has said, "Kindness is a language which the deaf can hear and the blind can see."[79] Kindness can touch our lives in almost miraculous ways.

Yes, expressing kindness is a way to touch lives and make a difference in our world. In fact, it can and does change our world one person at a time. Amelia Earhart has said, "The greatest work kindness does to others is that it makes them kind themselves."[80] I'm sure that many of the kindest people are probably those who have received a great number of kindnesses in their lifetime. Again, gratitude can be very influential. Because of all this, we get a deeper sense for how kindness is contagious and very powerful.

Cultivating Kindness

Even though there is a great deal of kindness all around us, it is true we all could improve in this area. We should always be on the lookout for how we can be kind. Each of us should spend time reflecting on the following two questions: (1) "How kind am I?" and (2) "What can I do to be more kind?"

Let's look at how we can cultivate kindness in our lives. First of all, we know as a fruit of the Spirit, kindness is highlighted as a very important quality for everyone to have as part of their godly nature.

We were born into the physical world where we live our everyday lives. For Christians, we have been born again and have become new creations (2 Cor. 5:17). The born again person delights in the things of God and seeks to do away with things of the flesh. Our purpose, feelings, desires, and understandings are fresh and diverse. We see the world differently. We seek to focus on the things of the Spirit.

Consider what the apostle Paul says in the following passages:

Romans 8:5:

> ...those who live in accordance with the Spirit have their
> minds set on what the Spirit desires.

Colossians 3:1–2:

> Since, then, you have been raised with Christ, set your hearts
> on things above, where Christ is seated at the right hand of
> God. Set your minds on things above, not earthly things.

We know that as we humble ourselves and pray, as we set our minds on
things above, and as we live for God, we enjoy the blessings of His power
in our lives.

As we seek to be obedient to the appeals in the Scriptures to be kind, we
must therefore dedicate ourselves to being persons of kindness. We know
that our actions flow primarily from who we are deep down inside us: our
values, beliefs, and character. Our kindness must result from intentional
efforts and not just from serendipitous encounters. We should be looking
for opportunities to be kind every day. We must strive for kindness to be
a way of life for us. We should seek to be eager to demonstrate kindness
in our daily lives. We should keep kindness on our daily agenda. We know
that the more we practice kindness, the more we will enjoy it and the more
it will become a habit.

One of the realities we should recognize is that we each have our blind
spots, things about us we don't see but others see. The truth is, sometimes
we are not even aware when we've been unkind. We all have our rough edges
that can unknowingly and unintentionally hurt the feelings of others and
discourage them. We would do well to ask others, especially our spouses and
good friends, to give us feedback when we are being unkind or insensitive
to other's feelings. However, when pointing out another's shortcomings, we
should do that with humble gentleness!

I've read in some of the studies about rudeness that people attribute
their lack of kindness to how busy and rushed they are on a daily basis.
Maybe if people would slow down and be more aware of their surroundings,
they would be more positive in their responses.

Random Acts of Kindness

There is a movement of kindness that has been spreading throughout the
world for some time now called "Random Acts of Kindness." There is even
an organization established to encourage people to perform random acts of

kindness called the Random Acts of Kindness Foundation. Its website can be found at https://www.randomactsofkindness.org/.

The term "random acts of kindness" is generally attributed to Anne Herbert who wrote "Practice random kindness and senseless acts of beauty" on a restaurant placemat. [81] The term refers to selfless acts, both large and small, that are committed unexpectedly, without prompting and with no apparent ulterior motive. Examples of this might include paying for a coffee for the person in line behind you at the coffee shop, helping a person cross the street, picking up trash on someone's yard, shoveling a neighbor's driveway when it snows, and so on. Loving and kind motives for generous acts do not seek to receive attention and commendation from others.

Pay It Forward

Many of us are familiar with the concept of "pay it forward." This was popularized by the movie by that name, which came out in the year 2000. Pay it forward acknowledges that the most powerful way to return someone's kindness is to pass kindness along to someone else. In this way, the acts of kindness shown to others can be multiplied over and over again.

This is not a new concept. It has been discussed and practiced by many over the generations. This underscores all the more the power and influence of kindness in our world.

Related to this idea is how kindness can have a boomerang effect. The more we give kindness, the more it comes back to us.

Conclusion

Hopefully we all look forward to succeeding in life and being welcomed into the eternal kingdom of our Lord and Savior Jesus Christ. This is based on the kindness of God. It merits a heart of gratitude and thankfulness, which finds expression in passing kindness on to others.

We need to always remember, "Wherever there is a human being, there is an opportunity for kindness."[82] Most opportunities for being kind come across our path in the ordinary course of our day. We don't need to look for the spectacular. These only come along infrequently. Few people ever have the opportunity to pull an unconscious person out of a burning car just before it explodes.

The apostle Peter encourages followers of Christ to be very active in serving others. He says in **1 Peter 4:10**:

> Each of you should use whatever gift you have received to serve others, faithfully administering God's grace in its various forms.

We all like it when we are shown kindness. We feel good when we show kindness to others. It's a win-win situation!

CHAPTER 8

Goodness

Be Rich in Good Deeds

"I cannot do all the good the world needs, but the
world needs all the good I can do."

—Jana Stanfield

We now come to goodness, the sixth "fruit of the Spirit" listed in Galatians 5:22–23. Goodness has a dual meaning and application. It relates to our standing before God and our interactions with other people. As we will see, goodness relates to one of God's highest priorities. Consider what the apostle Paul tells Titus, one of his converts, after talking about the hope we have of eternal life:

Titus 3:8:

> This is a trustworthy saying. And I want you to stress these things, so that all those who have trusted God may be careful to devote themselves to doing what is good. These things are excellent and profitable for everyone.

The reason why this is a high priority is because this is how love acts, and love is God's greatest attribute. One of God's prominent qualities is goodness. Doing what is good is an excellent way for Christians to showcase our godliness and dedication to God. It is prime evidence of our loving nature.

We all gain when others do good deeds for us. We are hardly ever closer to God's heart than when we are doing what is good.

Again, there are two ways of looking at goodness. One is about us being good and the other is about doing good deeds. Both are ways we can be very pleasing to God.

Goodness Defined

The goodness the apostle Paul is referring to in Galatians 5:22 is about doing good deeds to and for others. We understand this from the Greek word Paul used, which is **agathosune** (ἀγαθωσύνη), pronounced ag-ath-o-soo'-nay. [83] Agathosune is a word unique to the New Testament. It does not occur in secular Greek writing. It is a word that combines being good and doing good. It means kindness in actual manifestation, virtue equipped for action, and a bountiful propensity both to will and do what is good. It is intrinsic goodness producing generosity and a God-like state of being. It represents uprightness of heart and life.

Goodness relates to a heart that loves others and is willing to sacrificially serve the needs of others. It represents generosity which expresses itself in being useful and energetically doing good for the benefit others. Again, it relates closely to the idea of kindness as every good deed is an act of kindness.

Being Good

Being good is about possessing godly character from which our good actions flow. As Christians, we know that being good ultimately comes from God and what Jesus did for us on the cross. We are forgiven and are reconciled into a meaningful and right relationship to God. We choose to accept Jesus as our Lord and Savior, accept God's gift of salvation, and dedicate our lives to God. We are good because of the right relationship we have with God, which makes us good. Only Christians can be considered "good" in the sense that we are right with God. The righteousness we have comes from God. The apostle John relates to this in the following passage.

3 John 1:11:

> Dear friend, do not imitate what is evil but what is good. Anyone who does what is good is from God. Anyone who does what is evil has not seen God.

We also know we do good deeds when we show love to others and have caring qualities in our lives, such as kindness, grace, mercy, and gentleness. The truth is, anyone can do good deeds whether they are Christians or not. However, God wants us to be both good and to do good deeds.

God Is Good

We know from the Scriptures that God is good. Again, goodness is a part of God's nature. God can only do what is good. There are many passages that speak of this.

Psalm 34:8:

> Taste and see that the Lord is good; blessed is the one who takes refuge in him.

Psalm 107:1:

> Give thanks to the Lord, for he is good; his love endures forever.

Psalm 86:5:

> You, Lord, are forgiving and good, abounding in love to all who call to you.

Mark 10:17–18:

> As Jesus started on his way, a man ran up to him and fell on his knees before him. "Good teacher," he asked, "what must I do to inherit eternal life?"

"Why do you call me good?" Jesus answered. "No one is good—except God alone.

Could anyone imagine what it would be like if God was not good? Nothing pleasant comes to mind. Fortunately for all of us, goodness is an ever-present and unwavering part of God's character. Because of this, we can be assured that God's goodness is applied to all of us all the time. God is always consistent and true to His nature.

We often hear people say, "God is so good," when something good has happened to them. Now, this can create a distorted and false picture of God. We must realize that God is not just good when good things happen. God is good all the time. God is good even when bad and terrible things happen to people.

As we've discussed, there are groups of people whose scriptural doctrine embraces the notion that God is controlling all that happens. However, when bad and terrible things happen, how then does one explain God's goodness? If God has His hand in causing all the suffering around the world, how can the notion of God being good be associated with all of that? The problem with the concept of God taking control of everything is that God would then rightly get the blame for all the evil and terrible things that happen. Now, this does not fit with the character of God. How could God be considered good if He is doing bad and terrible things?

For example, what are we to think when a drunk driver kills a young family in a car crash? How are we to understand a situation in which a pre-teen child is viciously raped by an adult man? How are we to explain all of the murder, crime, child abuse, and so on in the world? Is the only way to explain this by putting the blame on God as being the one who caused that to happen? No! It is not, and it can't be.

A good God does not do evil deeds and does not cause evil to come upon innocent people. God hates evil. So when bad things happen, we must look elsewhere other than at God for the cause.

There are many other Christians who disagree with the doctrine of God being in control of everything and understand instead how "free will" is the reason why many bad things happen. We don't blame God. There is no glory in being associated with doing terrible things to innocent people. That is why we can say: "God is good, all the time. All the time, God is good."

There are many good books and articles by scholarly people regarding how we can understand suffering and evil in the world today without placing blame on God. They are easy to find and will concur with what I am saying here. I also have a chapter on this topic in my previous book, *Going Deeper with God, Addressing Challenging Issues in Our Relationship with God.*

Scriptures about Doing Good

We know there are many Scriptures appealing to Christians to do good deeds. Deep down, it's a part of our godly nature as we were created in the likeness of God. When we become Christians, after we are born again, we take on a new life and accept a new value system. We read in Acts 10:38 that Jesus went around doing good. As Christians, we see this as a clear example to follow. Consider the following passages appealing to us to do good deeds.

Ephesians 2:10:

> For we are God's handiwork, created in Christ Jesus to do good works, which God prepared in advance for us to do.

Galatians 6:9–10:

> Let us not become weary in doing good, for at the proper time we will reap a harvest if we do not give up. Therefore, as we have opportunity, let us do good to all people, especially to those who belong to the family of believers.

Matthew 5:14–16:

> You are the light of the world. A town built on a hill cannot be hidden. Neither do people light a lamp and put it under a bowl. Instead they put it on its stand, and it gives light to everyone in the house. In the same way, let your light shine before others, that they may see your good deeds and glorify your Father in heaven.

1 Timothy 6:17–19:

Command those who are rich in this present world not to be arrogant nor to put their hope in wealth, which is so uncertain, but to put their hope in God, who richly provides us with everything for our enjoyment. Command them to do good, to be rich in good deeds, and to be generous and willing to share. In this way they will lay up treasure for themselves as a firm foundation for the coming age, so that they may take hold of the life that is truly life.

Hebrews 13:16:

And do not forget to do good and to share with others, for with such sacrifices God is pleased.

Hebrews 10:24–25:

And let us consider how we may spur one another on toward love and good deeds, not giving up meeting together, as some are in the habit of doing, but encouraging one another—and all the more as you see the Day approaching.

Romans 12:21:

Do not be overcome by evil, but overcome evil with good.

Titus 2:7:

And as for you, brothers and sisters, never tire of doing what is good.

Titus 2:11–14:

For the grace of God has appeared that offers salvation to all people. It teaches us to say "No" to ungodliness and worldly passions, and to live self-controlled, upright and godly lives in this present age, while we wait for the blessed hope—the appearing of the glory of our great God and Savior, Jesus Christ, who gave himself for us to redeem us from all wickedness and to purify for himself a people that are his very own, eager to do what is good.

God wants the earth to be full of His goodness. He wants the earth to be full of people who do good deeds. God wants His people to do good to others as we represent Him here on earth. He also wants His people to have godly character from which goodness flows. We all, therefore, have goodness to share with others. We can be rich in good deeds.

Doing Good Is Personal

Doing good deeds requires us to be engaged with others. Sometimes this may have to be from afar. However, most of the goodness we are to do is a hands-on affair. It demands us to be up close and personal with others.

Doing good should come naturally and easily. Doing good energizes a Christian. Doing good reflects authentic Christians in word and deed. We should regularly see evidence of our good deeds. Our good deeds should be many, innumerable to count.

I heard a preacher once say that because the congregation was being asked to help people and non-profit organizations so frequently, he worried that people would experience "compassion fatigue." However, I see it quite differently. This congregation must have some of the most energized and joyful people around! Lending a hand to help those in need keeps us aligned with God's will and should make us all feel great. Any discouragement will likely come in feeling we wish we could do more to help.

Matthew 12:35:

A good man brings good things out of the good stored up in him, and an evil man brings evil things out of the evil stored up in him.

There are no exceptions to the requirement for doing good, no excuses. If one does not find themselves doing good regularly, something is wrong. One then must examine their heart. One would need to question their love and commitment to the Lord and their love for others.

Conclusion

Many attribute the following quote to John Wesley some 250 years ago. However, some challenge this, saying there is no evidence he actually said this. [84] Therefore, it would likely have to be attributed to "anonymous." Regardless of who said it, it is about a powerful charge relating to our obligation to do good deeds to others.

> Do all the good you can.
> By all the means you can.
> In all the ways you can.
> In all the places you can.
> At all the times you can.
> To all the people you can.
> As long as ever you can.

This is a formula for a happy life and a healthy society. This is a charge to help those in need, something very close to the heart of God. As we reach out and engage with others, so many possibilities are then opened for us to influence others for the Lord. As we can all imagine, this is best done in the context of a relationship with others versus with strangers. Something to think about as we strive to be as effective as we can for the Lord.

May God bless us in all of these endeavors!

CHAPTER 9

Faithfulness

Great Should Be Our Faithfulness

"Know therefore that the Lord your God is God; he is the
faithful God, keeping his covenant of love to a thousand
generations of those who love him and keep
his commandments."

—Deuteronomy 7:9

We now come to faithfulness, the seventh "fruit of the Spirit" mentioned in
Galatians 5:22–23. It is simply logical and appropriate to have this quality
mentioned as part of an important list like the fruit of the Spirit. Being
faithful is fundamental to living out our Christian faith and is a prime attribute of God. This aligns with how essential it is to maintain a healthy and
vibrant relationship with God.

In this chapter, we will look at this topic according to the following outline: (1) examine the case for faithfulness, (2) review the state of faithfulness
in America today, (3) acknowledge God's faithfulness to us, (4) clarify our
need to be faithful to God, and (5) emphasize our need to be faithful to others.

1. The Case for Faithfulness

The Greek word used for faithfulness is the word "**pistis**" (pronounced
as it looks) and means faith, belief, trust, confidence, and fidelity. [85] It carries the meaning of trustworthiness and reliability. It relates to the notion
of being faithful, trustworthy, dependable, and reliable.

It is safe to say that the apostle Paul in Galatians 5:22 was referring to Christians remaining faithful to God and to their Christian principles while also being faithful in all areas of life. This would include being faithful, trustworthy, and dependable in all relationships, including with spouses, friends, bosses, co-workers, clients, and customers. God is faithful in all He does, and we should strive to be the same.

The reality is that humans are not that great at being faithful and trustworthy. In fact, we all struggle with this to some degree. Many fail miserably.

If we think about it more deeply, we will see that the benefits of faithfulness are many and have a powerful impact in improving our lives and relationships with others. Faithfulness is a wonderful quality. Great blessings come from being faithful. Therefore, great should be our faithfulness. Being faithful, trustworthy, and dependable are very endearing and respected qualities. No one would ever say anything negative about faithfulness. Therefore, the need to pursue faithfulness is quite challenging and compelling.

On the other hand, being unfaithful, untrustworthy, and unreliable has many negative consequences for everyone involved. It can be a source of great pain and disappointment to ourselves and loved ones. No one views those qualities as honorable. No employers would hire someone they deem as untrustworthy and unreliable. People would not marry someone who says they plan to be unfaithful to them. No one would be proud to promote themselves as an unfaithful and untrustworthy individual.

When people get married, they, in a sense, "hire" the other person to be faithful to them. Love and faithfulness are the basic intentions and motivations for wanting to live life together. Being faithful is how we express our love, respect, and commitment to each other. This trust provides us the greatest sense of security and peace.

What kind of people would want to enter into a marital relationship where our spouse would only commit to 50 percent faithfulness? How can anyone really feel secure in the relationship when the pledge given in the marriage ceremony is a commitment to the other person for "as long as our love shall last?" What does this even mean?

Would anyone want to invest a lot of money in a business partnership with another person who says that they can offer a 50 percent commitment to be faithful and trustworthy to the working relationship?

Serious problems can occur from unfaithfulness in all kinds of relationships where trust is essential. Most careful people would do a good amount of research into the background of a person before agreeing to enter into such a trusting relationship. Often, when serious problems emerge in these relationships, one of the reasons can relate back to not doing a thorough enough effort to get to know the person really well. If the truth about the unfaithful person could have been known upfront, the other person probably would not have entered into such a trust-dependent relationship.

On the other hand, many people do enter into marital relationships with the intent and purpose to be forever faithful. Then, over time, things happen, and unfaithfulness occurs. What this highlights is the need to nurture love and commitment all along in the relationship. Everyone would do well to go through marital enrichment activities all throughout the marriage. There is much information on this that is easy to access.

2. Faithfulness in America

We all likely know that religious belief in America is declining. The evidence reveals that a growing number of people are not faithful to their religious beliefs. Consider the results of a study done by the Pew Research Center.

> The religious landscape of the United States continues to change at a rapid clip. In Pew Research Center telephone surveys conducted in 2018 and 2019, 65% of American adults describe themselves as Christians when asked about their religion, down 12 percentage points over the past decade. Meanwhile, the religiously unaffiliated share of the population, consisting of people who describe their religious identity as atheist, agnostic or "nothing in particular," now stands at 26%, up from 17% in 2009.

> Both Protestants and Catholics are experiencing losses of population share. Currently, 43% of U. S. adults identify with Protestants, down from 51% in 2009. And one-in-five adults (20%) are Catholic, down from 23% in 2009. Meanwhile, all subsets of the religiously unaffiliated population, a group also known as religious "nones," have seen their numbers swell. Self-described atheists now account for 4% of U. S. adults, up modestly but significantly from 2% in 2009; agnostics make up 5% of U. S. adults, up

from 3% a decade ago; and 17% of Americans now describe their religion as "nothing in particular," up from 12% in 2009. Members of non-Christian religions also have grown modestly as a share of the adult population. [86]

As we discussed previously, we know there is great unfaithfulness when it comes to marital relationships. There have been many studies on this. One done by a law firm in San Diego, California, reported the divorce rate in 2020 as follows:

- 41 percent of first marriages;
- 60 percent of second marriages; and
- 73 percent of third marriages. [87]

Many quote the divorce rate to be around 50 percent. However, this could be wrong. Harvard-trained social researcher and author, Shaunti Feldhahn, in her book, *The Good News about Marriage,* says that the data reveals a different story about the divorce rate. [88] Feldhahn states that the 50-percent figure was not based on hard data. She reports that the number came from projections of what researchers thought the divorce rate would become after states passed no-fault divorce laws. She writes, "We've never hit those numbers. We've never gotten close." According to her study, the overall divorce rate is around 33 percent.

Studies are also showing a falling rate of divorce in America, which is encouraging, although those rates are still high. [89]

As a country, we would do well to better understand why the divorce rate is so high and what could be done to substantially reduce that rate. Faithfulness is one essential variable.

What Can We Trust?

So, in what can we absolutely trust and depend on to be faithful in our world? A few things quickly come to my mind.

- We can absolutely trust in there being day and night.
- We can absolutely trust in there being time and, thereby, the ability to have a calendar.
- We can absolutely trust in gravity.

- We can trust in the North Star up in the sky.
- We can trust the predictable laws of nature.
- We can trust in mathematics.
- We can also trust that God will keep His promises and be true to His character. We should learn to take Him at His word. God is faithful, and great is His faithfulness.

Yes, more could be added, but unfortunately, that list would not be nearly as long as a list about what we can't depend on to be faithful.

3. God's Faithfulness

Let's refresh our minds about God's faithfulness. As no surprise to us, the majority of the references to faithfulness in the Bible refer to God's faithfulness. He is the gold standard when it comes to being faithful.

Let's briefly review some passages about God's faithfulness.

Exodus 34:6:

> And he passed in front of Moses, proclaiming, "The Lord, the Lord, the compassionate and gracious God, slow to anger, abounding in love and faithfulness..."

Lamentations 3:22–23:

> Because of the Lord's great love we are not consumed, for his compassions never fail. They are new every morning; great is your faithfulness.

Psalm 57:10:

> For great is your love, reaching to the heavens; your faithfulness reaches to the skies.

1 Corinthians 1:9:

> God is faithful, who has called you into fellowship with his Son, Jesus Christ our Lord.

2 Timothy 2:11–13:

> Here is a trustworthy saying:
> If we died with him,
> we will also live with him;
> if we endure,
> we will also reign with him.
> If we disown him,
> he will also disown us;
> if we are faithless,
> he remains faithful,
> for he cannot disown himself.

All of these passages are beautiful expressions of God's faithfulness. No genuine believing person could doubt God's love and faithfulness. We could not hope for any better from God. How blessed we are! Knowing we serve a loving, merciful and faithful God gives us much hope and comfort. Yes, we can trust in God's faithfulness!

On the other hand, can anyone imagine what it would be like if God were not always faithful and trustworthy? Fortunately, we don't even have to go there! Again, how blessed we are!

If there is a problem about God's faithfulness, it would come from the way people misunderstand God and how He relates to people today. All of this relates to what we've mentioned several times in this book about how there are some prominent churches whose doctrines emphasize God being in control of all that is happening, leading to unfulfilled expectations and disappointment with God.

4. Being Faithful to God

God is calling us all to have high levels of faith and commitment. We see this reflected in how we are to exhibit the fruit of the Spirit.

God wants us to love Him with all of our heart, soul, and mind (Matt. 22:37). He wants us to love our neighbors as ourselves. (Matt. 22:39). He wants us to rejoice always, pray continually, and give thanks in all circumstances (1 Thess. 5:16–18). God wants us to have peace with Him and for that peace to guard our hearts and minds (Phil. 4:7). God wants us to clothe ourselves in patience (Col. 3:12). God wants us to be kind and compassionate with each other (Eph. 4:32). God wants us never to be weary of doing good to others (Gal. 6:9). God wants to be able to say to us, "Well done good and faithful servant" (Matt. 25:23). God wants us to be found trustworthy (1 Cor. 4:2). God wants our gentleness to be evident to everyone (Phil. 4:5). God wants us to live self-controlled lives (Titus 2:12).

All of this, and more, underscores just how much God wants us to give Him our all when it comes to our faithfulness.

In Luke 18:8, Jesus asked His apostles, "When the Son of Man comes, will he really find faith on the earth?" Looking at the state of faithfulness today is not as encouraging a picture as many believers would have hoped it would be. As we've seen from the Pew Research Center study, God will find a checkered history and a disappointing current picture. On the one hand, there are many who devote their lives to God and sacrifice and suffer much for the Lord's sake. God is delighted by this. On the other hand, however, there are also many who give lip service to their faith. We even see some leaders in the faith go through a "de-conversion" process publicly as they proudly denounce their once-held belief in God.

We know the world has many, some say thousands, of different versions of Christianity, all claiming faithfulness to God and His doctrines. Far too many have been willing to change biblical truth to what suits them. There are many degrees of unfaithfulness and, unfortunately, it is rampant.

Be that as it may, we are called to be faithful to Him who is always faithful to us. As discussed earlier, this does not mean we have to be perfect to be accepted by God.

We are able to see that even God's best, the great people of faith described in the Bible, are not perfect even though God saw them as faithful. Everyone has been a disappointment to God at points in their lives. Everyone makes mistakes. God can use these to forward His purposes in significant ways. Consider Abraham, Isaac, Jacob, and David in the Old Testament. Consider the apostles Peter and Paul in the New Testament. All of these people give us hope and assurance that God can love, forgive, and use each of us even though we make mistakes.

God has given each of us skills, abilities, personalities, gifts, and talents that He expects us to use as we fulfill His purpose for our lives. He provides clear instructions in the Scriptures on the kind of life He wants us to live. We must be faithful in fulfilling our opportunities to do good and glorify God in all we do. This is the trust God has placed on us.

1 Corinthians 4:2:

> Now it is required that those who have been given a trust must prove faithful.

We know God wants our faithfulness. It is up to each person to respond in the right ways. All of us are going to stand in the presence of God and give an account of how we have used what He has given to us. Many will say that the Lord is not going to ask us how **much** we have done for Him, but rather, how **faithful** we have been to that which He wanted us to do.

5. Our Faithfulness to Others

We honor God when we are faithful, trustworthy, and dependable to other people. Our faithfulness is a way we can showcase our Christian commitment and values, glorify God, and bless others who come into our lives. We know we all have differing skills and abilities, and that is okay. We are just asked by God to use these as we can.

Jesus said in **Luke 12:48:**

> From everyone who has been given much, much will be demanded; and from the one who has been entrusted with much, much more will be asked.

We must realize that our financial strength is not all there is to our "muchness." This also represents our heart, talents, and abilities. We know when we become followers of Christ, we don't do so because we want the easy life. There will be much sacrifice and service required of us because of our faith. However, this is not God's way of testing or punishing us. It is God's way of blessing us. Just ask missionaries, pastors and ministers, foster and adoptive parents, Christian professional counselors, and those involved in all kinds of non-profit human service work. We all experience personal growth as well as satisfaction and joy from being engaged in making a difference in our world.

We must be risk-takers for the sake of the Lord and others. I think we all would agree that fear is not an adequate excuse for not being good stewards of the gifts and abilities God has entrusted to us. As in the parable of the talents (Matt. 25:14–28), some of the opportunities we have could be the chance of a lifetime. We all need the courage to take advantage of them when they arise.

Conclusion

Yes, we know that God asks a lot from each of us. When you think about it, He has to if He is going to want us to be like Him. If this was easy, then God would not be God.

I think of a story in the Old Testament that relates to the challenges we have today. As I understand it, what God wanted from Job was for him to remain faithful throughout all of his trials. Job did not have to understand the whys of his circumstances. In fact, God refused to address these. God just wanted Job to be faithful, and he was. I also think of Joseph who remained faithful through the ups and downs of his life only for things to work out in splendid ways (Gen. 37-50).

I'm sure that God wants the same kind of faithfulness from each of us. Spend some time thinking about this. How does your story of faithfulness lead to blessings in your life?

Let's close this chapter with the sentiments of the apostle Paul in **2 Timothy 4:7–8:**

> I have fought the good fight, I have finished the race, I have kept the faith. Now there is in store for me the crown of righteousness, which the Lord, the righteous Judge, will award to me on that day—and not only to me, but also to all who have longed for his appearing.

CHAPTER 10

Gentleness

A Strong Hand with a Soft Touch

"Let your gentleness be evident to all."

—Philippians 4:5

We now come to gentleness, the eighth "fruit of the Spirit" mentioned in Galatians 5:22–23. In many ways, all of the fruit of the Spirit highlight a softer side in how we are to interact with others. All of these qualities represent caring, inspiration, motivation, and empathy coming from the actions of one's heart. None of these qualities represent harsh and unloving ways, such as aggressiveness, coercion, harassment, intimidation, or force. Applying this softer side strengthens the quality of our interactions with others and is the best way to facilitate positive interpersonal relationships. This can then lead to better opportunities to make an impact for the Lord in others' lives.

Many say that gentleness is one quality most people don't think about very often. That is unfortunate. Can you remember when you last intentionally focused on this character trait? We all would do well to consider how we can be gentle in all of our relationships, especially with our spouses and children.

By being listed as a fruit of the Spirit, the apostle Paul has brought considerable attention to gentleness. Hopefully, as you apply this quality in greater ways to your lives, you will find that this will enhance the influence you have with others. Keep this in mind when you finish this chapter and see if what has been said inspires you to greater gentleness in your interactions.

God Is Gentle and He Wants Us to Be Gentle

Much of what we know about God's gentleness comes from what we learn from four major sources, (1) stories in the Old Testament, (2) what we hear about how Jesus interacted with others in the New Testament, (3) from biblical references to God's gentleness, and (4) from appeals to Christ followers. We see God's love, mercy, kindness, and gentleness reflected all throughout both the Old and New Testament Scriptures. There are many stories of how God responded to Moses and the Israelite people with compassion, patience, and gentleness.

Consider the following passages referring gentleness.

Isaiah 42:3:

> A bruised reed he will not break,
> and a smoldering wick he will not snuff out.
> In faithfulness he will bring forth justice...

Isaiah 40:11:

> He tends his flock like a shepherd:
> He gathers the lambs in his arms
> and carries them close to his heart;
> he gently leads those that have young.

We see gentleness reflected in how Jesus handled situations, such as the woman at the well (John 4) and with the woman caught in adultery (John 8). We read Scriptures specifically mentioning God's gentleness, such as in **Matthew 11:29:**

> Take my yoke upon you and learn from me, for I am gentle
> and lowly in heart, and you will find rest for your souls.

We read many Scriptures in the New Testament making strong appeals for us to be full of gentleness as well as having other qualities, which align with God's own nature.

Colossians 3:12:

> Therefore, as God's chosen people, holy and dearly loved, clothe yourselves with compassion, kindness, humility, gentleness and patience.

After talking about the love of money, the apostle Paul says to Timothy in **1 Timothy 6:11**:

> But you, man of God, flee from all this, and pursue righteousness, godliness, faith, love, endurance and gentleness.

Ephesians 4:1–2:

> As a prisoner for the Lord, then, I urge you to live a life worthy of the calling you have received. Be completely humble and gentle; be patient, bearing with one another in love.

Even while Paul was in prison, he was thinking of the way followers of Christ should act toward others with love, grace, and gentleness. So we see, it is clearly communicated in the Scriptures that God wants us to be gentle.

Gentleness Defined

The Greek word in Galatians 5:23 for gentleness is **prautés**, (πραΰτης), pronounced prah-oo'-tace. [90] It means mildness and gentleness. It also relates to the idea of humility and meekness (gentle strength), which expresses power with reserve and caution. Biblical gentleness involves having a humble heart and being kind toward others.

Some dictionaries define gentleness, in part, as being "mild-mannered" as we are polite and restrained in our behavior toward others. The Baker's Evangelical Dictionary of Biblical Theology defines gentleness as "sensitivity of disposition and kindness of behavior, founded on strength and prompted by love."[91]

To be gentle in the biblical sense requires the ability to control our reactions during all kinds of situations. Fortunately, many of our interactions occur in easy-to-handle, pleasant circumstances. Being gentle here is uncomplicated and simple.

At challenging times, such as when we are under pressure and dealing with difficult-to-handle situations, being gentle requires our inner strength. This comes from a healthy self-esteem, spiritual maturity, good judgment, and confidence. [92] Some people describe gentleness as controlled strength. Instead of being harsh, coarse, or demeaning to those who are aggressive and giving us a hard time, we need the ability to see beyond their outward behaviors and understand the inner frailty and weaknesses from which their behaviors are generated. Some negative reactions of people are not intended to be harsh or hurtful. Often times, it is just their normal style of interacting, although certainly not the best style. Sometimes the negative actions are subconscious defensive responses based on a person's insecurity. A gentle response is certainly more appropriate and helpful in these situations.

As we think of people having controlled strength, a prime example of this would be the fictitious character Superman! In the movie *Man of Steel,* which came out in 2013, Kevin Costner, who played his earthly father, was trying to teach Clark Kent gentleness and patience. [93] In one scene in the movie when Clark was a young child, there were boys his age who were harassing and bullying him. Clark wanted to retaliate, knowing he could easily defend himself, but restrained himself so as not to reveal his true strength. There were other times when Clark restrained himself from using his true strength at the urging of his father. His father wanted Clark to handle things this way because he did not think the time was right to reveal Clark's true strength and abilities. He didn't think humans were ready to be introduced to a super human person who was not from planet earth.

Although this is a story of fiction, it does demonstrate the principle of gentleness as controlled strength. We could apply this to real-life circumstances where powerful people restrain themselves from dealing with weaker people for the sake of gentleness. This power can be physical power, or it could be power that comes from position, status in life, or other circumstances or abilities. We should always endeavor to interact with others with self-control, calmness, and understanding. Possessing tact and thoughtful courtesy is a great strength so that we can de-escalate situations while helping others to retain their self-esteem and dignity.

We know Jesus was one with ultimate power and ability who showed great humility and restraint many times. We also see this in matchups between people where there is one who is clearly more powerful and capable being pitted against another person who is clearly less capable. This can play out in debates, one-on-one competitions, arguments, and the like. Gentleness is certainly required of the stronger ones who want to treat people with compassion and respect.

In graduate school to receive my master's degree in social work, one topic of importance discussed early in the first semester was the difference between aggressiveness and assertiveness. We were being trained to be assertive, not aggressive. This is because aggressiveness is an intimidating and harsh way of interacting with people. Aggressiveness can come from those who are insecure and are over-compensating for personal weaknesses. Aggressiveness is characterized as being harsh, hostile, argumentative, violent, destructive, and belligerent. This simply refers to being mean-spirited, uncontrolled, and not sensitive to the best way of relating to human beings. Assertiveness is based on one having a healthy self-esteem, a caring heart, self-confidence, and strength of character. Being gentle is a lot like being assertive.

Godly Gentleness Is Not Weakness

We must understand there is a big difference between how the world understands the idea of gentleness and how the Scriptures refer to it. In the secular world, we see many people who don't value gentleness and are under the misguided notion that gentleness reveals weakness.

As one example of how people don't value godly gentleness, consider some of those who are in leadership positions. They often believe that showing weakness can work against them. Many leaders want to be viewed as having strong, aggressive, and forceful personality traits. Many believe their strength must be expressed through firm and decisive action, which can include blunt and harsh treatment of others. They can be domineering, dogmatic and intimidating. They see this as the way to keep people submissive to their leadership. They want to be respected, but what happens often instead is that they are feared and disliked by others.

We all know of celebrities, professors, medical doctors, church ministers, politicians, experts in their field, and others who are very accomplished where fame, status, and influence can go to their heads. They may think of themselves more highly than they should and can easily become arrogant, selfish, and unlikeable, the opposite of gentleness.

An example of this scenario is depicted in the movie "Groundhog Day," which débuted in 1993. [94] Bill Murray's character, Phil Connors, was an up-and-coming weatherman in Pittsburgh. He had higher aspirations. He was arrogant, rude, a womanizer, and thought many people around him were beneath him. His attitude was that he should be treated in a special way. He described it as the need to "keep the talent happy." He was regularly impolite and offensive to the camera man assigned to him. Needless to say, many did not respect or like him. The camera man called him a "prima donna" (a show-off and brat). All of this was exaggerated to fit the comedy storyline for the movie, which was about Bill Murray's character living Groundhog Day over and over again, taking place in Punxsutawney, Pennsylvania. This experience caused him to reevaluate his behavior. He eventually shed himself of his arrogant ways and became sensitive, gentle, humble, thoughtful, and treated others well. People then began enjoying his company and respecting him.

All of these depictions are reflective of why God is so concerned about us being gentle to others. People are hurt, repelled, and turned off by arrogant, blunt, inconsiderate, and domineering people. The best way to connect with people is with gentleness, humility, kindness, love, patience, and other soft-side personal characteristics that Scripture emphasizes. So we can see how gentleness is the loving way to relate to others.

I believe this is the basis for the following passages.

1 Peter 3:15–17:

> But in your hearts revere Christ as Lord. Always be prepared to give an answer to everyone who asks you to give the reason for the hope that you have. But do this with gentleness and respect, keeping a clear conscience, so that those who speak maliciously against your good behavior in Christ may be ashamed of their slander. For it is better, if it is God's will, to suffer for doing good than for doing evil.

When we share the gospel with others, it's not just the words that count. People take into consideration our attitudes and character. In particular, if we don't have gentleness and respect toward those we are talking to, if we are domineering, rude, or disrespectful, the conversation we are trying to have will go nowhere. Treating people in any kind of setting without the utmost care and gentleness is not the way to be a good and effective representative of God and Jesus. Even when people don't seem to accept the gospel message we are sharing, we must reflect godly qualities at all times. That will speak positively to others even though they may not be ready or willing to accept our message at the time.

Consider **Galatians 6:1**:

> Brothers, if someone is caught in a sin, you who are spiritual should restore him gently.

Again, how would it be good to try to restore someone in a negative, harsh, demanding, and shameful way?

Consider **2 Timothy 2:22–26**:

> Flee the evil desires of youth and pursue righteousness, faith, love and peace, along with those who call on the Lord out of a pure heart. Don't have anything to do with foolish and stupid arguments, because you know they produce quarrels. And the Lord's servant must not be quarrelsome but must be kind to everyone, able to teach, not resentful. Opponents must be gently instructed, in the hope that God will grant them repentance leading them to a knowledge of the truth, and that they will come to their senses and escape from the trap of the devil, who has taken them captive to do his will.

This passage relates to what we've been saying. We must approach others with the gospel from a position of having a strong faith, a deep love for the Lord, and respect for them. We must instruct others, especially our opponents, gently without engaging in quarrels. We can see that being gentle and full of godliness is the best foundation for teaching others about Christ. By being negative, we can create a stumbling block for people who are in a search of the truth. It's likely they would be offended. We would then alienate them, and they may never engage with us again.

Proverbs 15:1:

> A gentle answer turns away wrath, but a harsh word stirs
> up anger.

So yes, how we treat others matters a great deal. It may be more impactful than what we are trying to communicate with words. We must not have the attitude that believes it is okay to say what you think and then let the chips fall where they may. Some insist they just want to say what they think. Others have friends. We all would do well to follow the apostle Paul's instructions in **Colossians 4:5–6**:

> Be wise in the way you act toward outsiders; make the most
> of every opportunity. Let your conversation be always full
> of grace, seasoned with salt, so that you may know how to
> answer everyone.

There is a quote that is often attributed to President Theodore Roosevelt, but this has never been verified. [95] The quote says: "People don't care how much you know until they know how much you care." Most people cannot be fooled. We can hurt the cause of Christ if we are not exhibiting the fruit of the Spirit.

Again, we must exhibit self-control to have gentleness and the other qualities of the fruit of the Spirit. Love is our motivation.

Gentleness with Those with Whom We Are Closest

We've looked at how gentleness is an important quality when we interact with a wide variety of people in our lives. We can also see how it can be extremely important in the special relationships we have, particularly between spouses and with our children. Gentleness may seem a little thing, but it can make a huge difference.

Gentleness between spouses can take many forms. One example is in how we address our spouses when they are irritable or in a bad mood for whatever reason and seemingly snap at us for no fault of our own. We may feel justified in snapping back in these situations. However, that rarely helps or works. Harsh words are often met defensively with harsh words.

I think there are many people who just seem predisposed to react in a harsh way. This, in part, has to do with previous life experiences. The responses may even be of a subconscious nature. This could be one reason the responses happen so often. Regardless of the explanation, what is the other spouse to do? This is when gentleness is needed. A gentle response will deescalate the situation. This takes self-control on the part of the responder. Treating the spouse with kindness, patience, gentleness, and understanding will help prevent the situation from getting worse. In reality, there is no need to snap back at a spouse in these situations. Maybe a long hug, saying, "I love you," and asking, "How can I be helpful?" can provide the grease to slide the other spouse out of a prickly mood.

This scenario can also give us guidance in how we treat children. When children are in a bad mood, their behavior can become irritable, obstinate, and as if they are almost asking for a fight. In reality, this could be a way they seek to have their need for attention and affection met at that particular moment. If a parent snaps back harshly at the child demanding compliance, it could easily escalate the situation. A soft approach may be the best way to handle many of these situations. Saying and doing nothing for a short time can help a child simmer down. Also, holding a child in your arms for a while can soften their attitude. Being positive and loving can help while employing distracting tactics. As we hear a lot from parenting coaches and other experts, we need to choose our battles carefully. Sometimes a little battle can turn into a big power struggle. This can be avoided. All of this can relate to gentleness also.

One of the great ideas to help parents be more effective in dealing with their children is to understand the concept of parenting styles. One style to avoid is often labeled the "autocratic" style. This may be reflective of the way the parent can mishandle the situation above.

The autocratic parent believes children should jump to obey their commands without exception or hesitation. They may give a directive and then count to three for the child to spring into compliance. They can often be heard saying, "Because I said so," when a child questions the reasons behind a demand. These parents operate from the perspective that "I set the rules; it is my way or the highway." They are not interested in what questions a child may have and give little regard to a child's opinion. They see little value in listening to the child's defense. We must realize that by listening to others, we show them respect and help them to feel important to us.

139

Autocratic parents are harsh in how they handle their children. This is one extreme style. The permissive parenting style is at the opposite extreme to the autocratic style. In between these styles is the best way to approach parenting. It is, in some respects, the middle ground between autocratic and permissive style, but it is much more. Children are treated with dignity and respect and allowed to express their thoughts, feelings, and needs. It does not mean they will get their way, but that they will get their say. This style is the firm but fair approach, establishing good communication while encouraging the child to take on more responsibility. I encourage all parents of young children to make sure they understand parenting styles and how important it is to choose to parent from the middle-of-the-road style. It is by far the best approach. It is the way of gentleness.

Times When an Autocratic Approach Is Necessary

We probably should acknowledge that some people are in professions where gentleness is not an overriding concern. Take the police who have to deal with unruly people, rioting, violence, threats against their lives, and so on. They often deal with the worst side of life in a community. There are times when they must shout commands and take control over situations, which are out of control. When a citizen is holding a gun in his hand and about to point it at a police officer, giving commands and demands is probably best in these circumstances. I've seen news stories of policeman trying to be gentle at first in dealing with this, but there is a definite time limit on the use of this approach. Shooting the person if he or she turns the gun toward the police officer could be the next step. So yes, there are times when gentleness is not the right approach. This is not to say that being gentle in dealing with people who are threatening to jump off a tall building is not a good strategy.

People who serve as principals and vice principals of schools often have to deal with unruly students in all kinds of situations. One is where a fight is about to break out. Sometimes firm and decisive action is needed. Then there are military people in war zones where they should not have to think about gentleness in handling situations. Seal teams on missions to rescue hostages or deal with terroristic threats and attacks are examples.

We can realize that even parents need to be firm and aggressive when telling a young child not to step into a dangerous situation where imminent physical harm could occur. Keeping our children safe sometimes requires a more blunt and forceful response.

These are examples of the kinds of situations that require exceptions to the gentle ways we seek to interact with people.

Conclusion

So, has this discussion of gentleness caused you to think of ways to apply it to your own life? Are you wondering how people think about you in this regard? Can you remember circumstances in which you were not as gentle as you should have been? We must think back and reflect upon situations in our past in order to grow and improve in the ways of gentleness and in all of the fruit of the Spirit.

I recently listened to a sermon on television on the topic of gentleness by an associate pastor at a large church in Southern California. He explained the true meaning of gentleness and applied many Scriptures to underscore the mandate we have as God's children to be gentle in our ways of interacting with others (as appropriate). He then made a comment I have heard many make, which I believe can be confusing and misguided. He said to "give our problems to God and let God deal with them." After that, he read some more Scriptures in order to encourage people to be gentle.

I see a little disconnect here. This relates to the notion I have tried to forward in this book about the partnership relationship we have with God. Why would there be so many Scriptures pleading for us to be gentle if we are just to give our struggles to God for him to handle them? I believe God wants us to learn how to be gentle. The Scriptures are putting responsibility on our shoulders, not God's.

We will grow in the ways of gentleness as we try harder each day to apply gentleness to our interactions. Yes, we can and should ask God and the Holy Spirit for strength and help. However, we should not ask God to step into our life, take us out of the way, and handle things for us by Himself alone. Again, the reason for this idea is based on the partnership relationship I believe we all have with God. We must remember that God is glorified when we learn to be capable and handle situations in life well.

CHAPTER 11

Self-Control

Inner Strength and Sound Judgment

"For the grace of God has appeared that offers salvation
to all people. It teaches us to say "No" to ungodliness and
worldly passions, and to live self-controlled, upright and
godly lives in this present age..."

—Titus 2:11–12

We now come to self-control, the ninth and final "fruit of the Spirit" mentioned by the apostle Paul in Galatians 5:22–23. Although listed last, this
in no way implies it is least in value. All the qualities listed as fruit are vital.
However, I wonder if a few can be elevated in importance over others. I
believe a case can be made that self-control is the second most important of
all. I would put love as the first and most vital quality without equal.

Without love, what we have to offer is meaningless (1 Cor. 13). Love
can transform our efforts into greatness. Love impacts us and our world in
tremendous ways. A case can be made that all of the fruit are reflections of
love. Self-control enables each of us to do what it takes to apply love and
all of the fruit with in our lives It seems to me that love is the motivation
for developing the fruit, and self-control is the common denominator that
facilitates our ability to do our part in developing the fruit. Just think about
it. How could we learn and apply all of these qualities without self-control?

The spiritual life is all about a balanced relationship between human
beings and God. I've made reference throughout this book that many people
think producing the fruit of the Spirit is all the work of the Holy Spirit with
no involvement from us. I've tried to make the case that this is misguided theology. I've tried to advance the notion that how we live out our Christian lives

is in partnership with God. It is us and God. God delights in our accomplishments which are based on how He has made us. He clearly gets all the glory.

The Scriptures are the most essential tool God uses to influence and change us. We read in **2 Timothy 3:16–17:**

> All Scripture is God-breathed and is useful for teaching, rebuking, correcting and training in righteousness, so that the servant of God may be thoroughly equipped for every good work.

We must respond to Scriptures with all of our efforts to apply them to our lives. As we read Scripture, meditate on Scripture, and try to live by the Scriptures, over time, it gets easier. This is a reflection of our commitment, dedication, growth, and spiritual maturity. How amazing it is that Christians can be thoroughly equipped for every good work! Much of our motivation comes from gratitude to God for what He has done for us, including His mercy, grace, the offer of salvation, and the promise of a home in eternity with Him.

Titus 2:11–14:

> For the grace of God has appeared that offers salvation to all people. It teaches us to say "No" to ungodliness and worldly passions, and to live self-controlled, upright and godly lives in this present age, while we wait for the blessed hope— the appearing of the glory of our great God and Savior, Jesus Christ, who gave himself for us to redeem us from all wickedness and to purify for himself a people that are his very own, eager to do what is good.

Here Paul mentions how being spiritually purified leads Christians to be eager to do what is good. We must be known for our good works. Excelling in applying the qualities mentioned as the fruit of the Spirit will result in producing a tremendous amount of good works. The truth is, the hope of salvation is a huge motivator. It leads to our eternal destiny. Being eager to do what is good comes from strong motivation and dedication.

I've been affirming that each of the nine virtues mentioned in Galatians 5:22–23 represent qualities of God's divine nature. Of course, these are not an exhaustive listing of God's qualities. We find in the Scriptures other qualities that also represent aspects of God's character and nature. All of these virtues represent how we should strive to live in order to become more like God.

Christopher J. H. Wright, in his book *Cultivating the Fruit of the Spirit: Growing in Christlikeness,* has said that he does not view self-control as an element of God's nature. [96] He says that God's purity, holiness, and perfection means that He does not need to exercise self-control. God does not have any sinful tendency within Himself. He does not get tempted to do anything wrong. He has no vulnerabilities. He always does what is right. God does not have to hold in check any evil or inappropriate desires. "God is light; in Him there is no darkness at all" as the apostle John said in 1 John 1:5. This is certainly something to wonder about here.

The first thought that comes to my mind in reaction to this is that God's characteristics are reflected in His abilities, not His vulnerabilities. God is perfect in all His character traits. Everything He does shows evidence of those qualities. Self-control characterizes and exemplifies God. He has self-control as evidenced by every decision He has ever made and how He shows patience and restraint. We understand God's character by who He is and what He does, not by what He doesn't have to do.

Now, that is not true for us. David Mathis, in his article, "Self-Control and the Power of Christ," has said that the idea of controlling one's own self, having self-discipline, presumes at least two things: (1) the presence of tendencies within us that need to be reined in and (2) the ability within us for drawing upon sources of power to restrain them. [97] Again, I believe this power comes from within us, including the strength and motivation that comes from our commitment and dedication to God. I also believe it comes from the help we receive from the Holy Spirit.

How We Define and Apply Self-Control

The Greek word for self-control in Galatians 5:23 is the word **egkrateia** (ἐγκράτεια), which is pronounced eng-krat'-i-ah. [98] This word means the seeking of self-mastery, self-restraint, and self-control. From this word, we can see that self-control is based on the premise that each person is responsible for how they live their lives. We hear terms, such as self-restraint, self-discipline, and self-regulated behavior. It involves exercising personal power over one's desires and passions. It's about living a well-balanced life within God's guidelines and parameters. It is based on the mind as the command central of a human's life. Our minds are expected to be used as we continue to learn new concepts and set boundaries where needed as we seek to take control over all aspects of our lives, including our inner desires, thoughts, words, attitudes, emotions, and behavior.

There's another Greek word used for self-control in the New Testament, and it is the word **sóphrón** (σὼφρων), which is pronounced "so'-frone."[99] It carries the meaning of sound mind, sound judgment, self-control, temperate, sober-minded, modest, and chaste. Self-control is the exercise of inner strength combined with sound judgment that enables us to think, do, and say things that are measured, evaluated, and pleasing to God.

Many Christian people see that self-control can be defined very simply: self-control is taking control over one's self. It is probably best defined as the governing of one's desires. There is a form of self-control that says "yes" to what we should do and "no" to what we should not do. Self-control is a way to battle and reign in the impulsive reactions to life's circumstances. Self-control is evidenced by the ability to effectively evaluate and understand key aspects of a situation in order to react thoughtfully and appropriately.

The above understanding of self-control can be contrasted to the idea that self-control is produced only by the Holy Spirit and not from man's efforts. Some adhering to this point of view have made the following comments.

- Though we are active in practicing it, we simply bear the fruit of self-discipline. We never produce it. [100]
- We ask the Holy Spirit to control us so that we can learn to control ourselves. [101]
- Here is a paradox of the Christian life: We must give up the control of self if we would gain self-control. [102]
- True self-control is not about bringing ourselves under our own control but under the power of Christ. [103]

All of the above may sound very spiritually insightful. However, the statements don't seem to make much logical sense when taking in the broader picture. They definitely seek to eliminate our responsibility in producing self-control. These statements are contrary to the Greek definitions of self-control in the Scriptures.

The Scriptures never say we are not to exercise self-control and just let God control us. On the contrary, the Scriptures say we must exercise self-control, and this relates to all aspects of our lives. When it comes to being accountable for our actions, emotions, attitudes, and so on, the responsibility rests upon us.

Our "Self" Needs to Be Controlled

Yes, there are many Scriptures that emphasize the need for us to display self-control. Self-control is the common denominator in our ability to obey Scripture and live our lives pleasing to God. The reality is, when it comes to having troubles, struggles, and challenges in life, many of these issues come from our personal weaknesses and vulnerabilities. A case can be made that each of us are the number one offender in our lives. We can be our own worst enemy. We are the cause of many of our problems. We are constantly at war with our sinful desires and are subject to the vulnerabilities that come because we are human beings.

How easily we can get caught up in self-centeredness and self-importance. How easy it is for us to yield to our temptations and let circumstances get the best of us. How easy it is for us to over-indulge and give in to our selfish and fleshly desires. The demand for self-control is a call to be on guard against these as much as we can. We must do our best while also seeking help from God and the support we can receive from other Christians.

The apostle Paul speaks to this in **2 Timothy 3:1–5**:

> But mark this: There will be terrible times in the last days. People will be lovers of themselves, lovers of money, boastful, proud, abusive, disobedient to their parents, ungrateful, unholy, without love, unforgiving, slanderous, without self-control, brutal, not lovers of the good, treacherous, rash, conceited, lovers of pleasure rather than lovers of God— having a form of godliness but denying its power. Have nothing to do with such people.

This is a harsh list. We can see that associating with people like that can cause us to be negatively influenced. However, if we are honest, we all can see some of ourselves in that list at times. According to Paul, we'd have to think twice about having anything to do with ourselves! At least, we should be aware of our own faults and weaknesses and do what we can to guard against these finding a secure and lasting foothold in our lives. We certainly don't want to be a bad influence on others.

We find another harsh list describing what could be even worse acts of the flesh in **Galatians 5:19–21**:

> The acts of the flesh are obvious: sexual immorality, impurity and debauchery; idolatry and witchcraft; hatred, discord, jealousy, fits of rage, selfish ambition, dissensions, factions and envy; drunkenness, orgies, and the like. I warn you, as I did before, that those who live like this will not inherit the kingdom of God.

Not only should we stay away from these people for fear of being influenced by them, but we also see that living fleshly lives like that will cause one not to inherit the kingdom of God. Why is this so? Because these are qualities greatly opposed to godly living, and God places the responsibility on us to live differently than what is in that list. Again, it demands extensive self-control on our part.

Paul emphasizes a similar message in **Ephesians 5:1–20**:

> Follow God's example, therefore, as dearly loved children and walk in the way of love, just as Christ loved us and gave himself up for us as a fragrant offering and sacrifice to God.

> But among you there must not be even a hint of sexual immorality, or of any kind of impurity, or of greed, because these are improper for God's holy people. Nor should there be obscenity, foolish talk or coarse joking, which are out of place, but rather thanksgiving. For of this you can be sure: No immoral, impure or greedy person—such a person is an idolater—has any inheritance in the kingdom of Christ and of God. Let no one deceive you with empty words, for because of such things God's wrath comes on those who are disobedient. Therefore do not be partners with them.

> For you were once darkness, but now you are light in the Lord. Live as children of light (for the fruit of the light consists in all goodness, righteousness and truth) and find out what pleases the Lord. Have nothing to do with the fruitless deeds of darkness, but rather expose them. It is

shameful even to mention what the disobedient do in secret. But everything exposed by the light becomes visible—and everything that is illuminated becomes a light. This is why it is said: "Wake up, sleeper, rise from the dead, and Christ will shine on you."

Be very careful, then, how you live—not as unwise but as wise, making the most of every opportunity, because the days are evil. Therefore do not be foolish, but understand what the Lord's will is. Do not get drunk on wine, which leads to debauchery. Instead, be filled with the Spirit, speaking to one another with psalms, hymns, and songs from the Spirit. Sing and make music from your heart to the Lord, always giving thanks to God the Father for everything, in the name of our Lord Jesus Christ.

Why would the apostle Paul plead with us so specifically to avoid sinful living and embrace godly living? It is because he places the responsibility on us to live rightly. We need to hear the details. Scriptures like this are addressed to followers of Christ. It's for us to hear for a purpose. We need to do the best we can to respond to the appeals made in this passage. We are not to delegate petitions like this by asking God to handle them for us. We are instructed to do many things in Scripture from the premise that we are responsible to learn and grow into maturity in these ways. Yes, it may not be easy in many circumstances. It may even feel overwhelming. However, we need to do our part. God will meet us there and help us.

Scriptures about Self-Control

Let's consider additional Scriptures specifically calling us to exercise self-control.

The apostle Peter speaks of self-control in **2 Peter 1:5–8**:

For this very reason, make every effort to add to your faith goodness; and to goodness, knowledge; and to knowledge, self-control; and to self-control, perseverance; and to perseverance, godliness; and to godliness, mutual affection;

and to mutual affection, love. For if you possess these qualities in increasing measure, they will keep you from being ineffective and unproductive in your knowledge of our Lord Jesus Christ.

1 Timothy 3:2 and restated in **Titus 1:7–8** regarding qualifications of elders and deacons (overseers):

Now the overseer is to be above reproach, faithful to his wife, temperate, self-controlled, respectable, hospitable, able to teach...

In Titus 2:3–8, the apostle Paul tells Titus to encourage older women to train their young women and young men to be self-controlled.

Proverbs 25:28 is often quoted in a spiritual discussion on self-control. It says:

Like a city whose walls are broken through is a person who lacks self control.

What is the message of that Scripture? Walls are for the purpose of protection and safety. To live without self-control is a risky way to approach life.

The above Scriptures regarding self-control do not give us an indication that we are not to strive to exercise self-control and just rely on the Holy Spirit to do this for us. Yes, we need to exercise a great deal of effort to achieve self-control. Again, it is a battle that includes the mind as a major player. One of the reasons why many do not succeed in cultivating the fruit of the Spirit and other qualities emphasized so much in the Scriptures is because it is not easy to do the mind work involved in developing godly habits. Concerted effort is needed. This includes time for thinking and meditating on the topics and issues which we need to work on. We need to evaluate ourselves each day to review how we are doing and what we can do better. We identify our strengths and weaknesses and strive to make improvements in all those areas. It's helpful to have a trusted friend in which we can receive encouragement and help on issues. It's when we live isolated lives that we have greater failures.

Control of the Tongue

As an example of our responsibility to be self-controlled, let's look at what James, the brother of Jesus, says about the control of our tongue (our speech) in **James 3:1–11**:

> Not many of you should become teachers, my fellow believers, because you know that we who teach will be judged more strictly. We all stumble in many ways. Anyone who is never at fault in what they say is perfect, able to keep their whole body in check.
>
> When we put bits into the mouths of horses to make them obey us, we can turn the whole animal. Or take ships as an example. Although they are so large and are driven by strong winds, they are steered by a very small rudder wherever the pilot wants to go. Likewise, the tongue is a small part of the body, but it makes great boasts. Consider what a great forest is set on fire by a small spark. The tongue also is a fire, a world of evil among the parts of the body. It corrupts the whole body, sets the whole course of one's life on fire, and is itself set on fire by hell.
>
> All kinds of animals, birds, reptiles and sea creatures are being tamed and have been tamed by mankind, but no human being can tame the tongue. It is a restless evil, full of deadly poison.
>
> With the tongue we praise our Lord and Father, and with it we curse human beings, who have been made in God's likeness. Out of the same mouth come praise and cursing. My brothers and sisters, this should not be. Can both fresh water and salt water flow from the same spring? My brothers and sisters, can a fig tree bear olives, or a grapevine bear figs? Neither can a salt spring produce fresh water.

This passage uses several powerful analogies to clearly show how impactful our words can be. It makes a strong and passionate appeal for us to choose our words carefully and only use them for good effect.

No one would want to be subject to a leader who does not have good self-control. No one would want to hire an employee who does not have a sufficient level of self-control. We all live under common sense requirements for exercising self-control. It is no surprise and, indeed, it should be expected that God would place this requirement on those of us who represent Him. Our motivation is to live our lives in ways which shows He makes a difference to us. We all can make improvements in taming and controlling our tongues. We must work hard on this.

Conclusion

To the world, our lives should reflect the kind of God we serve. So, what kind of reflection are we? Do we look like the Christ we proclaim as our Lord and Savior?

Other Scriptures Reflecting the Requirement for Self-Control

- Deny self, take up our cross and follow Jesus (Luke 9:23).
- Everyone who competes in the games goes into strict training. They do it to get a crown that will not last, but we do it to get a crown that will last forever (1 Cor. 9:25).
- Flee from all this (1 Tim. 6:9–11;1 Cor. 6:18).
- Take every thought captive. (1 Cor. 10:3–5).

Helpful Suggestions on Nurturing Self-Control

- We need to pray and ask for God's help.
- We need to cultivate connections with other godly people. We always need encouragement.
- We always need to be on guard. Establish and keep appropriate walls and boundaries.
- We benefit from being accountable. Have godly people in our lives to provide this to us.

- We need to know our limitations, temptations, and vulnerabilities. We need to be honest with ourselves in identifying what these are and do the best we can to guard against them.
- We need to fight the good fight. For our part, it's largely a battle of the mind. Our thought life is our first line of defense in the battle for self-control. Sound judgment is the beginning of self-control.
- We need to work at breaking bad habits and replacing them with good ones.
- We need to have some quiet time to meditate on all of this every day. Choose a good time of the day to do this.

It takes constant diligence to achieve the outcomes we desire. To exercise self-control requires us to discipline ourselves, set boundaries, and rule over our actions. A lack of self-control, on the other hand, leads to the free reign of fleshly, worldly patterns that end up exercising control over us. We must not let other people or circumstances choose the outcomes of our lives.

CHAPTER 12

Conclusion

The Character of God in our Lives

Maturity in the Christian life is measured by only one
test: how much closer to His Character have we become.

—Elyse Fitzpatrick

In this book we have examined a very important passage of Scripture, Galatians 5:22–23. This passage is an encouragement to clothe ourselves with nine qualities identified as fruit of the Spirit: love, joy, peace, patience, kindness, goodness, faithfulness, gentleness, and self-control. All of these qualities are aspects of the divine nature of God. Because of this, we all have a strong mandate to excel in these qualities. The greater these qualities are incorporated into our lives, the better our lives will reflect the character of God.

The scriptural mandate for developing the nine qualities of the fruit of the Spirit could not be any clearer. This is why these qualities are mentioned many times in the Scriptures. Given the charge to put on these qualities, we need to give this our best effort. Part of this includes doing what we can to keep these qualities always on our minds. I hope you have found this book helpful as you seek to strengthen these characteristics in your life.

The positive impact of these traits is without question or debate. When noticeably displayed in the everyday lives of Christians, others will take notice. This will help others see evidence of our authentic faith. This should enhance their willingness to hear our personal testimonies as we share our faith in God and Jesus.

I've presented information that provides a clear understanding of what each of the nine qualities (fruit) mean and what we can do to effectively apply them to our lives. My background in the social services field provides me a different and broader perspective to human behavior that can be uniquely applied to scriptural passages like this one. I hope you have noticed how I applied practical principles from my professional training and counseling experience to each of these qualities. We must remember that godly logic and common sense reasoning have a place in how we interpret Scripture.

This book began with disputing the premise many other writers on this passage of Scripture have adopted when they claim we have nothing at all to do with the development of the fruit of the Spirit in our lives. To them, it is totally the work and responsibility of the Holy Spirit. Now, this is a huge doctrinal disagreement with very serious implications.

I realize I brought up ideas that have challenged some doctrines that are held on to fondly by a large number of believers. I hope everyone can at least see that any doctrine I criticized was done with sufficient reasons and well thought-out objections which were supported clearly with Scripture and godly logic. These differences were what I believed had to be challenged as we searched for truth in this biblical study.

The reality in the broad Christian community is that there are many doctrinal differences that conflict with each other. This can be very confusing, especially for those new in the faith or for those searching to find God. The pursuit of the truth can be a challenging task considering all of the conflicting messages that abound about things spiritual. The search for the truth merits a deep review and analysis before deciding to embrace a controversial point of view. This is what I tried to provide in chapter two as well as in comments which were scattered throughout this book.

I've presented an alternative doctrinal view to the notion that many believe God is taking control of everything in our lives and world. I have called this view the partnership relationship I believe we all have with God. Now, I don't dismiss the Holy Spirit from having a role in the development of the fruit of the Spirit and in other godly qualities. However, I do believe Scripture describes the Holy Spirit's role in our lives as a helper to us, not one who dominates or controls us. We must have a proper understanding of this extra-human power.

As I mentioned earlier in the book, all of the fruit of the Spirit highlight a softer side in how we relate to others. These qualities represent persuasive, inspirational, and empathetic ways of interacting with one another. None of these qualities represent unloving or harsh ways, such as aggressiveness, coercion, harassment, intimidation, or force. This softer side facilitates positive and quality interpersonal relationships. Having these qualities shine in our lives is the best context for doing evangelism and making an impact for the Lord.

When you consider all nine of the godly qualities listed as fruit of the Spirit, which ones would not be important to you? Are there any that you would say are not worth having? In what context would any of these qualities not be of value? The point is, I believe we all would agree that each one of these attributes is incredibly important. We would not eliminate any of them as being unhelpful or irrelevant to living godly lives.

Considering these nine godly traits collectively, I sense they work together under this formula: love plus self-control enables us to have joy, peace, patience, kindness, goodness, faithfulness, and gentleness. All of these qualities are manifestations of love. Love is the motivator for developing these qualities, and self-control is the common denominator for how we use our abilities to facilitate, nurture, and apply these traits in our lives.

I've tried to make the case that love is the most important quality for us to have. The words and phrases we use to define love can take us to descriptions of God's character. We shouldn't be surprised by this. It reveals and reinforces the notion that God is love. Where we see love being expressed, we see God's nature in action.

Even as the best and most dedicated of us seek to incorporate the qualities of God's nature within ourselves, no one will ever reach the point of perfection. The reality is, we can't. We will never arrive at having these qualities fully developed. This will be an ongoing, forever pursuit.

Now, this does not mean we should be discouraged as we pursue these qualities. We should always keep doing our best and embrace this challenge as a worthy goal. Basically, this is part of the process of ongoing personal spiritual growth. If we were perfect and had nothing to work on in our spiritual lives, life would be boring. We all need meaningful goals to pursue throughout life. (How does this relate to the concept where some say God takes control of everything?)

Again, we should not get discouraged and disheartened by our failures and struggles. Our shortfalls should be used as added motivation to try harder and do better. We should find encouragement and satisfaction when we see ourselves improving in our quest. The objectives we seek should be based on improvement, not perfection. We must find joy in our improvements or else we would find no joy or motivation to continue. A meaningful life is an adventure of never-ending challenges.

Associated with this, I believe God delights in how we use our considerable talents and abilities. He is glorified by our skills, and accomplishments as these are really a reflection of Him and how He made us in His image. On the other hand, to look down upon the abilities of human beings is really a slam on God as if He couldn't create mankind with wonderful enduring qualities and abilities. Each of our accomplishments should be a source of encouragement, not in the sense of glorifying ourselves, but in enjoying the partnership we have with God where God ultimately gets all the glory.

I believe there is a multifaceted approach to effectively sharing the gospel with others. One aspect of this is the way we live our lives. This is where having the fruit of the Spirit is so relevant. I believe people take notice of how those of us who profess to be Christians live and behave in our daily lives. Christians are often under surveillance by those who know us. If how we act and relate to people does not match the values and beliefs we hold dear, others will look at us as hypocrites and not authentic Christians. If Christians don't display the fruit of the Spirit, if we are not kind, loving, patient, self-controlled, and so on, this can nullify the words we use to explain our faith. On the other hand, if these qualities are displayed prominently in our lives, then our lives become a powerful witness and confirmation of our faith.

Another aspect of sharing the gospel relates to the spoken message. It relates to having a way to effectively communicate the gospel to others. It relates to having answers to the questions people have about our faith and our ability to defend what we believe and why. We must establish a good relationship with those who are seekers and, from that context, engage with them in conversations about faith. Being a good example alone is not enough. We must use our words and share our message effectively as we engage in a teaching process.

Again, I suggest you read my first book, *Going Deeper with God: Addressing Challenging Issues in Our Relationship with God.*[104] In that book, I spend many chapters on how we can present the gospel effectively to people and lead them to Christ. I present persuasive reasons on why we should believe in God and then go into many dimensions of what a healthy relationship with God looks like. I also address conflicting messages being spread about what we can expect from God that is confusing to many people.

We now come to the end of our journey together. I hope reading this book has been a positive experience for you and that you are glad you completed this task. I hope it has challenged you to think more deeply about these topics and that you have grown spiritually. I know I have grown spiritually through this study.

As we pursue the efforts of godly living, we should keep the end in mind. Consider what the apostle Peter mentions in **1 Peter 1:8–9**:

> Though you have not seen him, you love him; and even though you do not see him now, you believe in him and are filled with an inexpressible and glorious joy, for you are receiving the end result of your faith, the salvation of your souls.

I Can Use Your Help!

Once a book has been written, the challenge all authors face is how to get the book known to those who would be interested in reading it. You can help! If you enjoyed this book, please tell others about it. Writing a positive review of the book at Amazon.com or where you have purchased this book would be very helpful. I spent over a year writing this book, believing God wanted me to do this. It can only bless the lives of others if it gets in their hands! Thank you for considering this!

If you'd like to contact me, you can reach me at this email address: goingdeeper with God806@gmail.com.

About the Author

Douglas Mead grew up in a suburb of Boston, Massachusetts. He attended college at David Lipscomb College in Nashville, Tennessee, for two years and then went to Abilene Christian University in Abilene, Texas, where he graduated with a double major in social work and psychology and a minor in Bible.

Doug spent his whole career working for Christian-based child and family service agencies. He first worked as a social worker for the Children's Home of Lubbock in Lubbock, Texas, for two years and then went to the University of Texas at Arlington, where he received his master's of science in social work (MSSW).

Doug then went on to work as the program director at a residential program for boys, Timothy Hill Children's Ranch in Riverhead, New York, for four years. He then served as the executive director of Christian Family Services of the Midwest in the Kansas City area for eleven years. That agency provided foster care, adoption, and counseling services. This is where Doug received his clinical license in social work and provided marriage, family, and individual counseling. He then went to serve as the executive director of Georgia Agape, Inc, in Atlanta, where he worked for twenty-one years until he retired. Georgia Agape provided foster care and adoption services. Doug had a small private counseling practice during this time.

While in Georgia, Doug was very active in an adoption advocacy group called the Georgia Association of Licensed Adoption Agencies. This is a statewide organization where he served several terms as president. He also served on the board of directors of two child and family service organizations. One was a statewide advocacy and networking organization in Georgia called "Together Georgia," previously named the "Georgia Association of Homes and Services for Children." He also served on the board for the "Christian Child and Family Services Association," a national advocacy and networking organization, which is now called "Network 1:27."

Over the years, Doug had been involved with churches in the communities where he and his family lived. He served as a deacon for two congregations, as a small group leader, and taught adult Bible classes. He also traveled to speak to churches each year to promote the work of the agencies he served. While in Georgia, Doug spoke over 500 times in the pulpit to over a hundred congregations throughout the state and taught many Bible classes. He also was a presenter at professional conferences on a variety of topics.

Prior to his retirement, Doug received several awards honoring his service and commitment to the field. One was the "Distinguished Service Award" from the Christian Child and Family Services Association. He also received the Lifetime Achievement Award from the Christian Child and Family Services Association. He received the "Gail Bayes Lifetime Achievement Award" from Together Georgia.

Doug has been married to his loving wife, Nancy, since 1976. They have two sons and daughters-in-law and four grandchildren. They both retired from their professional careers in 2016. They love retirement and the time they can spend with their grandchildren! Doug is also active in his home congregation, including teaching the adult Bible class from time-to-time. He also does regular pro-bono consulting for Agape Villages, Inc. in Northern California, a state-licensed and nationally accredited foster care and adoption agency. He is also the author of the book, *Going Deeper with God, Addressing Challenging Issues in Our Relationship with God.*

Endnotes

1   Norman L. Geisler and Ronald M. Brooks. *Come Let us Reason: An Introduction to Logical Thinking* (Grand Rapids: Baker Academic, 1990), 13, 19.

2   John MacArthur, "Fruit of the Spirit, Part 1," https://www.youtube.com/watch?v=5J0BaD5Zhag&t=1526s, May 24, 2018.

3   Definition of Eusebeia, https://biblehub.com/greek/2150.htm.

4   John MacArthur, "Fruit of the Spirit, Part 1," https://www.youtube.com/watch?v=5J0BaD5Zhag&t=1526s, May 24, 2018.

5   Michael Caputo, *The Fruits of the Holy Spirit: Understanding the Transforming Fruits of God's Spirit* (Self published by Michael Caputo, 2015).

6   Ibid, 163.

7   Ibid, 165.

8   Ibid, 165.

9   Gregory Dickow, *The Truth About the Fruit of the Spirit*, https://www.youtube.com/watch?v=q6XZRHhP57k&t=176s, March 12, 2020.

10 Michael R. Burgos, *Life Changers Church International and Pastor Gregory Dickow*, http://www.biblicaltrinitarian.com/2014/05/life-changers-church-international-and.html, May 17, 2014.

11 Kevin Cotter, "Did Francis Really say, Preach the Gospel at all Times and, if Necessary, use Words," October 4, 2011, (https://focusequip.org/did-francis-really-say-preach-the-gospel-at-all-times-and-if-necessary-use-words/).

12 Stephen R. Covey, *The 7 Habits of Highly Effective People: Powerful lessons in Personal Change* (New York: Simon & Shuster, 2004) 30.

13 Definition of Simile, *Webster's New World College Dictionary*, Fourth Edition, (Macmillan USA, 1999) 1336.

14 Definition of Metaphor, *Webster's New World College Dictionary*, Fourth Edition, (Macmillan USA, 1999) 905.

15   Definition of Parable, *Webster's New World College Dictionary*, Fourth Edition, (Macmillan USA, 1999) 1043.

16   Definition of Analogy, *Webster's New World College Dictionary*, Fourth Edition, (Macmillan USA, 1999) 50.

17   Definition of Hyperbole, *Webster's New World College Dictionary*, Fourth Edition, (Macmillan USA, 1999) 701.

18   Definition of Personification, *Webster's New World College Dictionary*, Fourth Edition, (Macmillan USA, 1999) 1075.

19   Definition of Anthropomorphism, *Webster's New World College Dictionary*, Fourth Edition, (Macmillan USA, 1999) 60.

20   Definition of Paradox, *Webster's New World College Dictionary*, Fourth Edition, (Macmillan USA, 1999) 1043.

21   Definition of Metaphor, https://www.grammarly.com/blog/metaphor/, January 14, 2021

22   Definition of Karpós, https://biblehub.com/greek/2590.htm.

23   Compelling Truth, "What is the Fruit of the Spirit?" https://www.compellingtruth.org/fruit-of-the-Spirit.html.

24   Kathy Howard, "What are the Fruit of the Spirit?" https://www.crosswalk.com/faith/spiritual-life/what-are-the-fruit-of-the-spirit.html, March 1, 2021.

25   Dr. Bill Bright quoted in the book: Thomas E. Trask & Wayde I. Goodall, *The Fruit of the Spirit: Becoming the Person God Wants You to Be*, (Nashville, TN: Emanate Books, 2000), ix.

26   Thomas E. Trask & Wayde I. Goodall, *The Fruit of the Spirit: Becoming the Person God Wants You to Be*, (Nashville, TN: Emanate Books, 2000), xxv.

27   Ibid, xxvi.

28   Don Steward, *How the Holy Spirit Works in our Lives* (Published by Educating Our World (EOW), www.educatingourworld.com), 113.

29   Moody Bible Institute, *The Person and Work of the Holy Spirit*, https://www.moodybible.org/beliefs/positional-statements/holy-spirit/.

30   Jerry Bridges, *The Fruitful Life: The Overflow of God's Love Through You*, (Colorado Springs, NavPress, 2006), 9.

31 Dr. Bill Bright, "Why Do You Need The Filling of the Holy Spirit?" (Adapted from the Book: Transferable Concept: How You Can Be Filled with The Holy Spirit, (Bright Media Foundation and Campus Crusade for Christ International, 2009), taken from an internet article, https://www.cru.org/us/en/train-and-grow/transferable-concepts/be-filled-with-the-holy-spirit. 2.html.

32 Andrew Wommack, "The Sovereignty of God," (YouTube Video at https://www.youtube.com/watch?v=4KybB3UECmM, March 17, 2010).

33 Definition of Sovereign, *Webster's New World College Dictionary*, Fourth Edition, (Macmillan USA, 1999), 1372.

34 Definition of Despotés, https://biblehub.com/greek/1203.htm.

35 Definition of God's Sovereignty, https://www.gotquestions.org/God-is-in-control.html.

36 Christopher Ash, *Where Was God When that Happened: and Other Questions about God's Goodness, Power and the Way He Works in the World*, (UK:0333 123 0880, The Good Book Company, 2016), 13, 14, 15, 16, 17, 18 and 19.

37 Definition of Parakletos, https://biblehub.com/greek/3875.htm.

38 Definition of Pléroó, https://biblehub.com/greek/4137.htm.

39 C. S. Lewis, *God cannot ravish, He can only Woo*, https://www.inspirationalstories.com/quotes/cs-lewis-he-cannot-ravish-he-can-only-woo/.

40 Christina Daniels, "How Many Times Does the Bible Mention Love?" from the Adorned Heart Website, August 17, 2020, (https://www.adornedheart.com/how-many-times-does-the-bible-mention-love/).

41 Jesus trek, https://jesustrek. live/2019/10/17/the-north-star-of-the-bible/.

42 Ken Weliever, *The Preacher Word*, https://thepreachersword.com/2017/04/26/great-verses-of-the-bible-john-316/.

43 Jimmy Couch, https://www.quora.com/Why-is-John-3-16-one-of-the-most-important-and-therefore-the-most-memorized-verses-in-the-Bible.

44 What Does John 3:16 Mean? https://www.gotquestions.org/John-3-16.html.

45   Ken Weliever, *The Preacher Word*, https://thepreachersword. com/2017/04/26/great-verses-of-the-bible-john-316/.

46   Ken Weliever, *The Preacher Word*, https://thepreachersword. com/2017/04/26/great-verses-of-the-bible-john-316/.

47   Ken Weliever, *The Preacher Word,* https://thepreachersword. com/2017/04/26/great-verses-of-the-bible-john-316/.

48   What Does John 3:16 Mean? https://www.gotquestions.org/John-3-16.html.

49   Definition of Kardia, https://biblehub.com/greek/2588.htm.

50   Definition of Psuché, https://biblehub.com/greek/4771.htm.

51   Definition of Dianoia, https://biblehub.com/greek/1271.htm.

52   Definition of Kainos, https://biblehub.com/greek/2537.htm.

53   Definition of Joy, *Webster's New World College Dictionary*, Fourth Edition, (Macmillan USA, 1999), 773.

54   Definition of Chara, Precept Austin (https://www.preceptaustin.org/ joy_-_chara).

55   Definition of Chara, Bible Hub/Interlinear (https://biblehub.com/ greek/5479.htm).

56   Theopedia (https://www.theopedia.com/joy).

57   Stephan G. Hofmann, Ph. D, Ann Asnaani, M. A., Imke J. J. Vonk, M. A., Alice T. Sawyer, M. A. and Angela Fang, M. A., *The Efficacy of Cognitive Behavioral Therapy, A Review of Meta-Analysis*, https:// www.ncbi. nlm. nih. gov/pmc/articles/PMC3584580/, July 31, 2012.

58   Daniel David, Ioana Cristea and Stephan G. Hofmann, *Why Cognitive Behavioral Therapy is the Current Gold Standard for Psychotherapy*, https://www.ncbi. nlm. nih. gov/pmc/articles/ PMC5797481/, January 29, 2018

59   Definition of Peace, *Webster's New World College Dictionary*, Fourth Edition, (Macmillan USA, 1999) 1058-1059.

60   Definition of Eiréné, https://biblehub.com/greek/1515.htm.

61   Ibid.

62   Stephen R. Covey, *The 7 Habits of Highly Successful People: Powerful lessons in Personal Change*, (New York: Simon & Shuster, 2004), 102-153.

63 Definition of Diókó, https://biblehub.com/greek/1377.htm.

64 Definition of Eirénopoios, https://biblehub.com/greek/1518.htm.

65 Mind Tools, "Hurry Sickness, 10 Ways to Overcome Constant Panic and Rush," https://www.mindtools.com/pages/article/how-to-beat-hurry-sickness.htm.

66 Definition of Patience, *Webster's New World College Dictionary*, Fourth Edition, (Macmillan USA, 1999) 1055.

67 Definition of Makrothumia, https://biblehub.com/greek/3115.htm.

68 Kira M. Newman, *Four Reasons to Cultivate Patience, Greater Good Magazine: Science-Based insights for a Meaningful Life*, April 4, 2016, https://greatergood. berkeley. edu/article/item/four_reasons_to_cultivate_patience#:~:text=The%20study%20of%20patience%20is, ulcers%2C%20diarrhea%2C%20and%20pneumonia.

69 Ray Williams, "The Rise of Incivility and Bullying in America," October 20, 2014, https://www.linkedin.com/pulse/20141020121023-1011572-the-rise-of-incivility-and-bullying-in-america.

70 Vince Raison, "Acts of Kindness: Why Helping Strangers is Good for You," https://www.huffingtonpost. co. uk/entry/acts-of-kindness-why-helping-strangers-is-good-for-you_uk_595ba1ace4b02734df343b82.

71 Definition of Chrēstotēs, https://biblehub.com/greek/5544.htm.

72 Unknown, https://www.askideas.com/kindness-is-the-root-of-all-good-things/.

73 Richard Carlson, https://www.goodreads.com/quotes/467735-choose-being-kind-over-being-right-and-you-ll-be-right.

74 Oscar Wilde, http://www.amyreesanderson.com/blog/the-smallest-act-of-kindness-is-worth-more-than-the-grandest-intention-oscar-wilde/#. YhU4LOjMKUk.

75 Jean-Jacques Rousseau, https://www.brainyquote.com/quotes/jeanjacques_rousseau_406107.

76 Robert Stand, *Kindness*, (Green Forest, AR: New Leaf Press, 2021), 37.

77 Ralph Waldo Emerson, https://www.inc.com/peter-economy/25-quotes-about-kindness-that-will-inspire-you-to-make-a-difference-and-be-happy.html.

78   Mother Teresa, "Goodreads" online at this link, https://www.goodreads.com/quotes/18064-kind-words-can-be-short-and-easy-to-speak-but.

79   Mark Twain, "The Apocryphal Twain: Kindness is a Language the Deaf Can Hear," Center for Mark Twain Studies on line at the following link: https://marktwainstudies.com/apocryphaltwainoptimism/.

80   Amelia Earhart, https://quotefancy.com/quote/959787/Amelia-Earhart-The-greatest-work-that-kindness-does-to-others-is-that-it-makes-them-kind.

81   Anne Herbert, "About: Random Acts of Kindness," online at the following link, https://dbpedia.org/page/Random_act_of_kindnessand also corroborated as asserted in the following link: https://quoteinvestigator.com/2017/11/22/kindness/.

82   Lucius Annaeus Seneca, https://www.trafalgar.com/real-word/kindness-proverbs/.

83   Definition of Agathosune, https://biblehub.com/greek/19.htm.

84   Kevin M. Watson, "Wesley Didn't Say it: Do all the good you can, by all the means you can...," 2013, https://Kevinmwatson.com/2013/04/29/wesley-didn't-say-it-do-all-the-good-you-can-by-all-the-means-you-can/.

85   Definition of Pistis, https://biblehub.com/greek/4102.htm.

86   Pew Research Center, "In U. S. , Decline of Christianity Continues at Rapid Pace," October 17, 2019, https://www.pewforum.org/2019/10/17/in-u-s-decline-of-christianity-continues-at-rapid-pace/.

87   Wilkinson & Finkbeiner, Family Law Attorneys, "Divorce Statistics: Over 112 Studies, Facts and Rates for 2020," 2020, https://www.wf-lawyers.com/divorce-statistics-and-facts/.

88   Shaunti Feldhahn, *The Good News About Marriage*, (Colorado Springs, CO: Multnomah Books, 2014).

89   Wendy Wang, "The U. S. Divorce Rate Has Hit a 50-Year Low," November 10, 2020, https://ifstudies.org/blog/the-us-divorce-rate-has-hit-a-50-year-low.

90   Definition of Prautés, https://biblehub.com/greek/4240.htm.

91 Definition of Gentleness, *Baker's Evangelical Dictionary of Biblical Theology*, https://www.biblestudytools.com/dictionary/gentleness/.

92 Bible dictionary, https://www.biblestudytools.com/dictionary/gentleness/.

93 *Man of Steel*, Warner Bros. Pictures, 2013.

94 *Groundhog Day*, Columbia Pictures, 1993.

95 Theodore Roosevelt Quotes, https://www.theodorerooseveltcenter.org/Learn-About-TR/TR-Quotes?page=112.

96 Christopher J. H. Wright, *Cultivating the Fruit of the Spirit: Growing in Christlikeness*, (Downers Grove, Illinois: InterVarsity Press, 2017), 143.

97 David Mathis, "Self-Control and the Power of Christ," October 8, 2014, https://www.desiringgod.org/articles/self-control-and-the-power-of-christ.

98 Definition of Egkrateia, https://biblehub.com/greek/1466.htm.

99 Definition of Sóphrón, https://biblehub.com/greek/4998.htm.

100 Steven Lawson, "What is Self-Discipline?" https://www.ligonier.org/posts/what-self-discipline.

101 Christopher J. H. Wright, *Cultivating the Fruit of the Spirit: Growing in Christlikeness*, (Downers Grove, Illinois: InterVarsity Press, 2017), 144.

102 Steven Lawson, "What is Self-Discipline?" https://www.ligonier.org/posts/what-self-discipline.

103 David Mathis, "Self-Control and the Power of Christ," October 8, 2014, https://www.desiringgod.org/articles/self-control-and-the-power-of-christ.

104 Douglas L. Mead, *Going Deeper with God, Addressing Challenging Issues in Our Relationship with God*, (Meadville, Pennsylvania: Christian Faith Publishers, Inc. , 2021).

CPSIA information can be obtained
at www.ICGtesting.com
Printed in the USA
JSHW060031150822
29241JS00006B/147